ep sport

Tennis

Sue Rich

D1371751

A & C Black · London

First published in 1989 by
A & C Black (Publishers) Ltd
35 Bedford Row, London WC1R 4JH

ISBN 0 7136 5667 0

A CIP catalogue record for this book is
available from the British Library.

Photograph acknowledgements
Cover photograph courtesy of
Action Plus; all other photographs by
Michael Chittleborough.

Typeset by Pindar (Scotland) Ltd, Edinburgh
Printed and bound in Great Britain by
M & A Thomson Litho Ltd,
East Kilbride, Scotland.

CONTENTS

INTRODUCTION

When you mention the game of tennis most people associate it with Wimbledon, the greatest tennis show on earth. To most school children who hold a tennis racket, it is the thought of going to Wimbledon one day which inspires them to play.

Tennis actually originated as an outdoor version of the game called Real Tennis. Although no one person can claim to have 'invented' tennis, Major Walter Clopton Wingfield, an Englishman, patented a game in the early 1870s which he called 'sphairistike', and which later came to be known as 'Lawn Tennis'. The game was originally played by the leisured classes, usually as a garden party activity, and was an instant success. It was not until around the time of the First World War that tennis really began to spread. The British press then started to devote space to it, and with the advent of professional coaches and the development of tennis courts, the game soon began to expand.

Tennis has often been thought of as a sport for the upper classes, but today it is played in most countries of the world. Its popularity has been greatly encouraged and influenced by extensive media coverage, particularly by television and the showing of 'live' tennis all over the world via satellite. With the added new technology which has helped to transform tennis court surfaces, and the boom of indoor facilities, the game can now be played all year round.

Tennis is a wonderful sport and a highly complex and fascinating game, which can provide a most enjoyable form of exercise for people of all ages and all levels of ability. Tennis is a sport for life. Although initially quite difficult for the beginner, the introduction of short tennis, a scaled-down version of tennis, has added to the boom in tennis with young people. Short tennis is played on a short tennis court, or on a badminton court which is the same size. The rackets are smaller than standard tennis rackets and are made of plastic; the indoor ball is a foam ball and the outdoor ball is slightly harder, but still softer than a tennis ball. The sport is primarily for young children aged 5–10 years who are just learning ball and racket skills, but it is also an excellent teaching aid for older children and adults. Having mastered the skills of short tennis, they can then proceed to tennis in its 'real' form.

Today, many young players make their mark in the game at a very early age; for example, Boris Becker won Wimbledon twice before he was 20 years old, and in the women's game Steffi Graf was Olympic gold medallist and winner of the Grand Slam at the age of 19. Coinciding with younger players reaching such heights so soon, there has been a marked increase in the popularity of the game of short tennis, enabling young children to mimic their idols in a controlled, simple way. Coupled with the new technology in manufacturing rackets for children, the game has certainly been made easier to play from the ages of five or six years.

This book is aimed at teaching you the basics of tennis and giving coaches, teachers and players helpful insights into these fundamentals so that the game of tennis can be fun and played enjoyably for many years to come. Don't forget, tennis is a sport for life.

Note: Throughout the book players and coaches are, in the main, referred to individually as 'he'. This should, of course, be taken to mean 'he or she' where appropriate.

The author in full flight on the service!

1

THE GAME OF TENNIS

Tennis is a highly complex game involving two players (singles) or four players (doubles), and is all about trying to get in the right place at the right time to play the correct shot, made more difficult by an opponent who is trying to hit the ball away from you. The idea of the game is to hit the ball in such a way that either your opponent cannot retrieve it or you force him into making an error.

THE COURT

The court itself usually has both singles and doubles markings on it (see Fig. 1).

When a combined doubles and singles court is used with a doubles net for a singles match, the net should be supported to a height of 1.07 m (3 ft 6 in) by 'singles sticks' which are positioned 0.914 m (3 ft) outside the singles court on each side. In both cases, the net should be 0.9 m (3 ft) high at the centre.

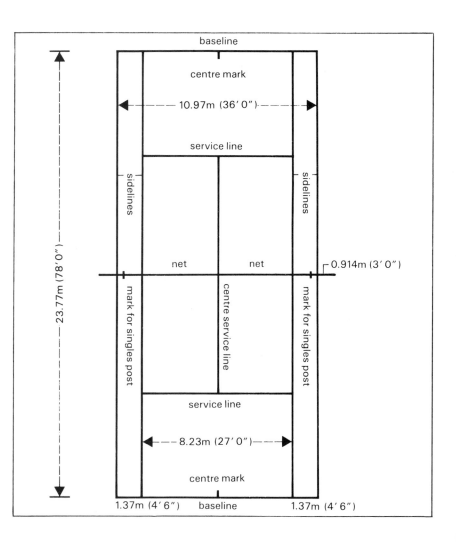

RULES OF THE GAME

The rules of the game are fairly complicated (and are explained in *Know the Game Tennis*, published by A & C Black).

Initially, players toss a coin or spin a racket and the player who wins the toss can choose one of four alternatives:

a elect to serve – in which case his opponent has the choice of ends

b elect to receive – in which case his opponent has the choice of ends

c choose ends – in which case his opponent may elect to serve or receive

d request his opponent to make the choice.

The loser of the toss may select whatever remains available to him, i.e. service, return of service, or side. Players are then allowed a five minute warm-up, after which play begins.

Fig. 1 Left *The court and its dimensions. The singles court is 8.23 m wide and 23.77 m long. The doubles court includes both sidelines and is 10.98 m in width.*

Fig. 2 Right *A player serving from the right side of the court has to serve the ball into area A. If serving from the left court, the player aims the ball to land in area B.*

The server begins serving from the right-hand court and has to try to get the ball into area A (see Fig. 2), the service box. If the ball lands in, the rally begins and the point is played out until one player makes an error, or fails to retrieve the ball. Should the first serve fail (called a fault), the server has a second chance. If this, too, fails, a double fault is called and the server loses the point.

The server then serves from the left court into area B, and, again, the point is played out. The server continues to serve from alternate sides until a game is completed.

SCORING

The scoring for tennis can often be confusing for a beginner, because it does not follow a logical pattern. The present scoring system originates from Real Tennis in which

fifteen, thirty and forty are all minute points on a scoring clock.

At the start of the game both players have a score of 'love' (0–0). The server's score is always called out first: if the server wins the point, the score is 'fifteen love' (15–0); if the receiver wins the point, the score is 'love fifteen' (0–15).

If the server wins the first and second points, the score is 'thirty love' (30–0). Should both players reach 'forty points' each (40–40), the score is called 'deuce' and the winner of the game is the first person to win two points in a row from deuce. If the server wins the first point after deuce, the score is 'advantage server'. If he then wins the next point, it is game to the server; however, if the receiver wins the next point, the score returns to deuce.

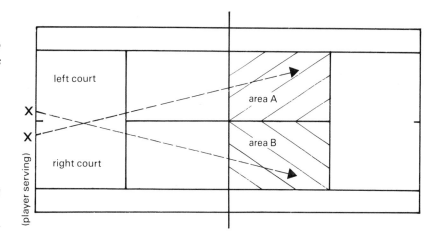

At the conclusion of the first game, the players change ends and subsequently do so on every odd numbered game.

If the score at the end of a set is 6–4, i.e. an even number of games, the change of ends is made after the first game of the next set. A set is usually called when one player reaches six games. If the score reaches five games-all then one player has to be two clear games ahead, e.g. 7–5, 8–6 or 9–7. Most matches today include a tie-break scoring system which operates at six games-all. This prevents situations such as that in the first round of Wimbledon in 1969, when Pancho Gonzales played Charlie Pasarell in a marathon match of 112 games. It lasted 5 hours and 12 minutes, and started one day and finished the next with the score 22–24, 1–6, 16–14, 6–3, 11–9 to Gonzales.

Most matches today are the best of three sets, although some men's matches are the best of five sets. The tie-break is generally played in the first two sets only of a three-set match and the first four sets of a five-set match (although some tournaments, notably the U.S. Open, play a tie-break in all sets).

WINNING AND LOSING POINTS

Tennis is all about the skills and tactics employed by a player in order to win points. Unfortunately, many points are also lost! With practice, a player can develop his ground strokes, service, volleys, tactics and physical and mental strengths in preparation for the game, so that he can use these skills to win points and to force his opponent into making errors.

How to win points

Points are won as follows:

a by hitting the ball in such a way that it bounces twice in your opponent's court before he can hit it

b by hitting a 'shot' that your opponent cannot reach

c by serving the ball in such a way that your opponent cannot return it, or so that the ball touches him or anything he wears or carries (except in the case of a let)

d by forcing your opponent to make an error.

Unfortunately, there seem to be far more ways for a player to *lose points* than to win them! The more obvious ways of losing points are listed below (for details of less obvious ways, consult a rules book).

How to lose points

Points are lost as follows:

a by letting the ball bounce more than once before returning it over the net

b if the ball in play hits the ground, a permanent fixture (see or another object outside the lines which bound your opponent's court

c by volleying a ball from behind the baseline and making a bad return (if a good return is made the rally continues)

d by catching the ball when standing out of court before it has bounced; the ball must bounce before an 'out' decision can be made

e by volleying a ball before it has crossed the net (the one exception is, for example, on a very windy day when your opponent plays a drop shot and the ball rebounds back over the net onto his side. You can then reach over the net and play the ball, provided you do not touch the net)

f by throwing your racket at the ball in an attempt to hit it

g by touching the net, posts, singles sticks, cord or metal cable, strap or band or ground in your opponent's court while the ball is in play

h once the ball is in play it is not allowed to touch you or anything you wear or carry, except your racket.

Try to keep to winning points – it is much easier to understand!

2

EQUIPMENT

SHOES

Shoe manufacturers have designed a full range of predominantly white shoes for different court surfaces: indoor carpet, clay, grass, etc. Find a pair which gives you a good fit and plenty of ankle support, is slip-proof and hard-wearing, and is specific to the surface you play on. Ideally, a good tennis player will have two or three different pairs of shoes with different soles, e.g. for indoors, wet courts, grass, clay and hard courts.

CLOTHING

The traditional tennis attire is white, and many clubs and tournaments still adhere to this convention. Recently, there has been a boom in the tennis clothing market and a

wide range of colours can now be bought. When purchasing an item of clothing, whether it be a dress, skirt and top or shorts, make sure it is comfortable and allows plenty of freedom of movement. Absorbent material is very useful as you are

likely to sweat freely when playing tennis. Some players carry a small towel attached to their shorts to mop up perspiration, and many players wear sweat bands or head bands. In extreme heat, do not be afraid to play in a sun hat.

This young player, clothed in white, is wearing a dress in which she can move comfortably. A headband is worn to keep her hair under control, and it also helps prevent perspiration dripping into her eyes.

TENNIS BALLS

As a result of modern technology, there are a variety of different balls and colours. The most popular colour is yellow, which is now used at Wimbledon (after many years of the traditional white ball). Some tennis balls are specifically designed for hard-wearing surfaces.

New tennis balls are expensive, but the better your standard of play, the more essential it is to play with good quality balls. Once a ball loses its cover and becomes bare, it just flies through the air and makes it very hard for a player to develop any rhythm and control.

THE RACKET

Before embarking on the purchase of a tennis racket it is a very good idea, particularly for the beginner, to seek the advice of a tennis professional or expert on the type of suitable equipment.

With the advent of new technology, a wide variety of rackets are available on the market to cater for the needs of young children, the beginner, the club player and the professional. As the racket is the most important piece of equipment, it is vital to find one that suits you. It is well worth spending a little more money to get the right racket with correct weight, grip size and stringing for your own needs as a tennis player.

The photograph below shows the short tennis rackets and three different types of short tennis balls suitable for children of 5–10 years (or for older children and adults as a teaching aid to tennis).

The second photograph shows a variety of sizes of rackets suitable for the young player, the average player, the county player and the professional.

Weight

The weight of a racket can range from 300 g (11 oz) to 377 g (13 oz). Modern graphite rackets are generally light and will tend to be marked as: USL (ultra superlight), ESL (extra superlight), SL (superlight), L (light), LM (light medium) and M (medium).

Obviously, a young, physically small player would be more suited to a superlight or light, rather than a medium racket. If a junior has a racket that is too heavy, it will tend to drag the wrist down and make it very hard for the player to develop a good technique.

Stringing

Basically, there are two types of strings: gut (natural) and nylon (synthetic), although there are varieties of each. Gut is vastly more expensive than nylon, but is more elastic and yields more to the ball. Many professional players use gut, and change the tension of the strings to suit their style of play and perhaps the court surface on which they are playing. Gut is very sensitive to damp conditions and, as a result, most average players tend to use synthetic strings. They are cheaper and can be used in any

Short tennis rackets and three different types of short tennis ball: the indoor foam ball, the intermediate ball (used inside or outside) and the outdoor ball (as seen from left to right).

A variety of different rackets to suit all ages and standards. From left to right: a short tennis racket, a mini racket, a beginner junior racket, a top quality junior racket, a full size top class racket.

weather conditions. The tension of the strings will depend partly on the specific recommendations of the racket manufacturer, and also on the individual's own style of play.

Grip size

This is measured by the size of your hand. A small hand needs a small grip size and, conversely, a large hand needs a larger grip. The grips on a full size racket range from size 1 (with a circumference of $4\frac{1}{8}$ in) to size 6 ($4\frac{3}{4}$ in). There has been a tendency recently for players to use a smaller grip size than in years gone by. A rough guideline is: you should be able to grip the racket firmly, and your thumb and forefinger should just be able to touch each other round the grip.

3 THE GRIP

The first fundamental which you need to know is *How to hold the racket*. The way you do this will influence the angle of the racket face, where you actually meet the ball, and what happens when the strings contact the ball.

Ever since tennis began, there have been varying views on the subject, and the grip is a topic for continuing controversy. The answer is simple, though: use the grip which works best for your needs, so that you can hit the ball with optimum balance of power and control. If a grip is limiting performance, it ought to be changed. For example, if a player hitting a backhand continually hits the ball out of court because he is using a forehand grip, then it is only logical to alter the grip and, hence, the angle of the racket face.

There are three grips which could be described as basic: Eastern, Continental and Western. The majority of coaches teach the Eastern forehand and backhand, although many clay court players favour a slightly Western forehand grip.

THE FOREHAND GRIP

The Eastern forehand grip

The term 'Eastern' originates from the fact that the grip was used by many players in the Eastern part of the United States, on clay courts where the ball bounced at a pleasant waist height. Most players use this grip, because the palm of the hand is behind the racket handle, making it an ideal grip for balls of varying heights. It is a natural extension of the hand, and makes it easy to achieve maximum strength.

To find this grip, hold the racket in front of you, supported at the throat with your non-gripping hand in an edgeways position. Place your gripping hand flat on the racket strings, slide it down the handle until you come close to the end, and then take hold of the racket as if shaking hands. When gripping the racket, try to spread your fingers out a little, and make sure your thumb is wrapped round the racket.

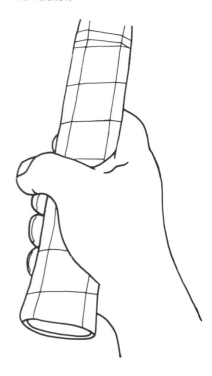

Fig. 3 The Eastern forehand grip or shakehands grip. Here the palm of the hand is behind the handle of the racket.

12

The Western forehand grip

This grip originated on the hard cement courts of California, where the ball bounces very high. It is an ideal grip for a high-bouncing ball or a waist-height ball. The problem comes with a low ball either on the baseline or at the net, because the hand is underneath the handle, making it difficult to get the racket head down for low balls.

Fig. 4 The Western forehand grip. The palm of the hand is underneath the handle of the racket. This grip is useful for achieving heavy topspin and is not generally recommended for beginners.

The semi-Western forehand grip

This is a slight variation of the above grip: the hand is not quite so far underneath the racket. This grip is ideal for balls above the waist, and leads to aggressive forehands, but it does require more of an open stance position for successful impact and control. The actual contact point tends to be closer to the body than in the case of the Eastern grip.

THE BACKHAND GRIP

A variety of different grips are used on the backhand, but this mainly depends on whether you play a single- or a double-handed backhand.

The Eastern backhand grip

The basic grip for the single-handed backhand is an eastern backhand grip. Here the heel of the hand is partly on the left bevel of

This young player is seen hitting a forehand drive with a semi-Western grip.

The Eastern backhand grip as seen from above.

the racket (i.e. your knuckle is on top of it). This position is reached by turning the hand inwards a quarter of a turn from the forehand grip. The thumb should be positioned diagonally across the back of the handle. This is a strong grip because it provides strength behind the handle, but still allows a good degree of flexibility.

The two-handed backhand grip

When first hitting a backhand, a beginner or young player might very easily just add his free hand to the racket (next to his Eastern forehand grip) for convenience. This makes it a very simple shot for the novice, as there is no grip change.

Both the left and right hands have forehand grips.

As the standard of the player progresses, he should be encouraged to change to a more flexible grip. Some players will move on to a chopper, or Continental grip, while others will change even further to the Eastern backhand grip.

Whichever grip is used on the two-handed backhand, the top hand (i.e. that added to the racket) should always make a forehand grip, and it is essential to have both hands close together and touching each other.

The advantages of a double-handed backhand are that greater strength can be achieved with two hands than with one, there is more flexibility and strength for control of the swing, and it is easier to disguise passing shots. If the grip is changed to a backhand one, it is easier to play a one-handed backhand if the need arises. This shot is often required on wide balls, at both the baseline and the net.

The main disadvantage of two hands is obviously the short reach,

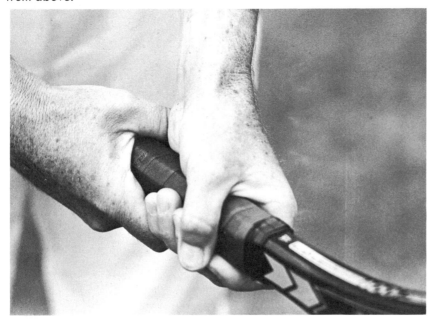

The two-handed backhand grip, which is often used by beginners. Here the forehand grip is maintained with the bottom hand (the hand nearest the end of the handle) and the free hand is just 'added' to the racket.

and the player also has to get closer to the ball which, in turn, means he needs good footwork about the court. The actual hitting area is different from the conventional one-handed backhand.

Most of the top players who play double-handed, with the notable exception of Jimmy Connors, tend to change their grip to a backhand one. It is hard to hit controlled topspin without a grip change, and Connors tends to hit a fairly flat or sliced backhand, as opposed to Wilander, who changes his grip and uses a lot of topspin.

I would recommend a grip change if you play with a double-handed backhand, and always do some practice on single-handed backhands in case you need them in a match.

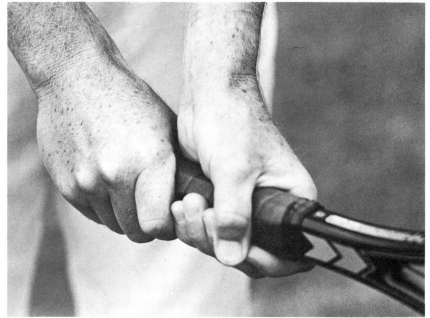

Above *The two-handed backhand using the chopper grip with the bottom hand.*

Right *Many advanced players change the grip of the bottom hand to a full Eastern backhand grip. This makes it easier to hit with topspin.*

THE CHOPPER OR CONTINENTAL GRIP

The Continental grip originated in Europe, specifically in France — where the soft dirt courts produced a low bounce. In the case of ground strokes, this grip can be used for both forehand and backhand, and is particularly good with low-bouncing and waist-height balls. However, it does prove difficult to achieve good racket face control on high balls. It also requires a very strong wrist and more precise timing than for the Eastern grip. It is not really recommended for the average player hitting ground strokes. This grip is found by finding the central position between the 'shake hands' of the forehand and the Eastern backhand, so that the palm of the hand is on top of the racket.

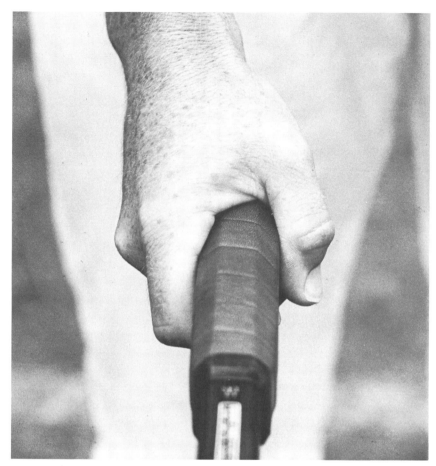

The chopper grip as seen from above.

MAKING A CHANGE OF GRIP

Do not alter a grip for the sake of a change, but if you decide that a particular stroke will work more effectively with a slight alteration, then do so. You must then be prepared to put in plenty of time on the practice court, as it will take thousands of practice shots before you will feel comfortable with your new grip. This is one of the reasons for trying to encourage the correct grips at the earliest age possible. If you have been playing tennis for years and you are content with the results from the grips you use, then a change is probably not worth all the effort.

4 THE BASIC STROKES

Technique can be defined as 'the method of performance'. In tennis terms, 'style' of play is talked about. This means the movements that are carried out in order to execute the specific skills of tennis. Players need to have a basic understanding, or technical knowledge, to carry out skills successfully. It does not follow that everybody has the same style; far from it: although the games of Boris Becker and Mats Wilander, for example, are totally contrasting, these men have the same basic technical knowledge from which they have built their own individual styles.

The aim of this section is to provide an understanding of basic techniques, including ground strokes, the service and return of service, net play, the lob and the smash.

THE FOREHAND DRIVE

The forehand drive is generally the first stroke learned in tennis, probably because it is the easiest to master; once you can hit a forehand and underarm serve (similar to the forehand swing), you can play a game. The easiest grip to use is the Eastern forehand.

Start in the ready position, i.e. the position that is going to make it easier for you to get off the mark quickly, so that you can get to the right place at the right moment for hitting the ball.

When in the ready position, support the racket with your free hand at the throat (unless two-handed), and start with a relaxed forehand grip. Your feet should be shoulder width apart, your body bent over towards the racket head, your knees slightly bent and 'springy', and your eyes focused on your opponent. If you are hitting ground strokes, the ready position is approximately one metre behind the centre of the baseline. A beginner might well stand inside the baseline.

From here, take the racket back early. As soon as you see the ball leave your opponent's racket and come to your forehand, start to turn

The ready position for groundstrokes. The player is standing just behind the baseline, near to the centre mark.

at the hips and shoulder, so taking the racket back. The backswing should not be too high or too long, and should be in the form of a small loop. The weight should now be on the back foot. The height of the racket will depend on the height of the oncoming ball.

A smooth connection is then made between the backswing and the forehand swing. The swing is from low to high, thus giving the ball lift. As the racket swings through, the weight is transferred onto the front foot. The swing should finish high and in the direction in which you want the ball to go. Use your free hand for balance.

The hitting area, or contact point with the ball, is slightly in front of the leading hip and at a comfortable distance from the body (arm's length away). It is essential to have a firm grip on contact with the ball. Maintain your balance throughout the stroke, and on completion return to the ready position.

The forehand drive shadowed. *Start in the ready position.*

The first movement is a turn with the hips and shoulders, so taking the racket back.

Step into the shot by transferring your weight forwards.

In order to hit a solid forehand you must have a sound knowledge of ball sense application, i.e. hitting a ball as it is falling after the top of the bounce; hitting the ball between knee/waist height; hitting the ball a comfortable distance from your body.

The arc of a falling ball will tend to encourage the correct groove on the forward swing. An absolute beginner would not be able to, or even be expected to, attempt all of these points in one go. It might be more sensible to think of the stroke in the terms:

turn: by turning the body, the racket will be taken back
step: transfer your weight onto the front foot
swing: try a low to high swing.

Once a player has the basic ability to contact the ball, the stroke can be improved by working on one or two of these points at a time.

The backswing is connected to the forward swing by a shallow loop. The point of contact with the ball is at a comfortable distance from, and slightly in front of, the body.

Finish with a high follow-through in the direction you want the ball to go. Note that the player is balanced here.

If a semi-Western forehand grip is used, when the weight is transferred into the shot, the stance will be semi-open with the hitting area/contact point now level with the front foot, but still a comfortable distance away. This grip is easier to use with high-bouncing balls, so it would be better to play the ball above hip height. It is far more difficult to hit low balls.

Typical mistakes on the forehand

a Wrong grip (if the backhand grip is used, the ball will be played too late).

b Playing the ball too close to the body.

The forehand drive in action. *Corinna prepares early, taking the racket back as soon as she sees the ball is coming to her forehand side.*

Her eyes are focused on the ball all the time. Her weight is transferred forwards.

c Hitting the ball too early (beginners in particular should try to hit a falling ball).

d Letting the ball drop too low.

e Preparing too late with the takeback.

f Hitting the ball too late (often related to poor preparation).

g Loss of balance during the stroke.

h Stance too open.

i Poor follow-through, with racket wrapped around the neck.

j Not watching the ball for long enough.

The racket comes through in a shallow loop and makes contact with the ball in front of the body.

The follow-through is high and in front of the body.

THE BACKHAND DRIVE

Many people dread the backhand, but once mastered, it is one of the easiest shots to hit.

The one-handed backhand

As before, start in the ready position. As soon as you see the ball coming to your backhand side, change the grip to an Eastern backhand. Prepare early and make 'sure you get a good turn at the shoulders. When the racket is taken back, it should be supported with your free hand (i.e. with the left hand, if you are right-handed). This hand only comes off the racket just before impact.

The backhand drive shadowed. Start in the ready position. Change the grip to an Eastern backhand.

The first movement is a turn at the hips and shoulders, so taking the racket back.

The weight is then transferred onto the front foot. Note the player steps forwards and not parallel with the baseline.

Step into the shot, thereby transferring the weight onto the leading foot. The swing is one from low to high and so gives the feel of 'lift' on the backhand. Ensure a good follow-through in the direction you want the ball to go. The contact/hitting area should be slightly in front of the leading foot and, again, at a comfortable distance from the body.

Try to keep the grip firm on impact. Maintain balance throughout the stroke and on completion return to the ready position.

It is much easier to hit a backhand if, as outlind above, you hit the ball as it is falling, at approximately knee/waist height.

The backswing is connected to the forward swing by a shallow loop. The point of contact with the ball is a comfortable distance from, and slightly in front of, the body.

The follow-through is high and in front of the body. The player here is balanced.

The backhand drive in action.
Sue prepares early using the
Eastern backhand grip.

As the ball approaches, Sue makes
a good shoulder turn; her body
weight is about to be transferred
forwards. Although the takeback is
high here, the racket head will
come below the ball as the
backswing and forward swing are
connected.

Sue has now transferred her weight
forwards and is perfectly balanced
just prior to making contact with the
ball at waist height. Note how she
watches the ball and maintains
good concentration.

Contact with the ball is made just in front of the body.

The follow-through is high and in front of the body, and the player is balanced.

The two-handed backhand

This shot has the same preparation and swing as the one-handed backhand, but both hands are next to each other on the grip, and the contact point/hitting area tends to be level with the front hip.

When deciding whether to use two hands or one hand on the backhand, it is essential to work out whether you are just copying a player or whether it is actually a natural stroke to you. If it is not a natural shot, or if you are not particularly quick around the court, you will be better off playing one-handed.

The two-handed backhand is especially useful for players who are not physically strong enough to use one hand, as the two hands add strength to control the racket face and swing, and there is more power

The two-handed backhand shadowed.
Start from the ready position. The hands are close to each other on the grip.

Turn at the shoulders and hips, so taking the racket back.

when hitting the ball. The limitations are that it cuts down your reach, both on the baseline and at the net, and it is therefore necessary to get into a really good hitting position to make a solid shot – the ideal situation which is not always possible in competition.

The beginner tends just to add his free hand to the racket without changing his grip. As the stroke develops, it is an idea to modify the grip to a backhand one, and then if the player so wishes he could easily change to a one-handed backhand.

With the introduction and success of short tennis and the availability of smaller rackets for young players, there will be a tendency once more for the young to use single-handed backhands.

The point of contact with the ball is slightly in front of and at a comfortable distance from the body (this will be slightly closer than with a single-handed backhand).

The follow-through is high and in front of the body. Note how the arms are not tucked into the body which would cramp the shot.

Typical faults on the backhand

a Wrong grip (particularly with the one-handed backhand when the grip is not turned round far enough).

b Grip not changed quickly enough, or slipping on impact.

c Grip is turned round too far (so that the ball ends up in the bottom of the net!).

d Poor preparation (racket not taken back early enough).

e Ball played late (ball ends up in the sideline).

f Not enough shoulder turn (no power in the backhand).

g Racket not supported on takeback with free hand (often leads to droopy racket head).

h Ball hit too early or too low (try to hit a falling ball).

i Player gets too close to the ball.

j Poor follow-through.

The two-handed backhand in action.
Tim has prepared early and transfers his weight forwards. His eyes are focused on the oncoming ball.

Contact with the ball is made at the side and in front of the body as the backswing is connected to the forward swing with a low to high action.

k Angle of racket face wrong on impact.

l Wrist and grip not firm enough on impact.

m Poor footwork – not stepping forwards to the ball, which means the player will be off balance when striking the ball.

The follow-through is in front of and away from the body.

THE SERVICE

The service is probably the hardest shot for the beginner to master. However, it is well worth spending time on the serve, as it is the most important shot in the game. If you cannot serve, you cannot play a game!

Why is it so many people suffer from 'stage fright' when serving? It is probably because the shot involves two distinct actions: placing the ball in the air, and hitting it. Tennis is one of the few sports in which you have to put the ball in motion and then hit it – unlike golf, for example, where the ball is stationary.

There is a great deal of satisfaction in hitting a good serve, and even more pleasure when the ball does not come back! One of the keys to good serving is staying relaxed and letting your body take over. If you tense up prior to serving, it is highly probable that you will not serve well and as a result it is unlikely that you will play to your full potential.

There are basically three types of serve: flat, topspin and slice. Let's take an indepth look at the technique for the flat serve (the variations will be discussed later).

For the beginner who has just mastered the forehand drive, it is quite sensible to use the basic forehand grip. In the initial stages, the idea is simply to get the serve into the correct box using a reasonable action. Once the beginner has a simple throwing action, the grip should be refined to the proper service grip, i.e. a chopper (Continental) grip. The chopper grip makes it easier to achieve greater racket head speed and to hit with controlled spin (topspin or slice), and allows greater flexibility. Many professional players turn their grip even further round to the backhand in order to impart more spin on the ball.

The service is the one shot over which you can take your time. You place the ball up and you hit it. All other shots are dependent on how your opponent hits the ball, but this is the moment when *you* are in complete control. If you can put in a good serve you can easily set yourself up to win the point.

Start in a sideways position, with your front foot pointing slightly towards the net post and the back foot parallel with the baseline. When serving in a singles match, stand near the centre mark, as this position represents the shortest distance between you and the opponent's service box, and thus is ideal for hitting a flat serve. In doubles, stand about half-way between the centre mark and the singles sideline.

Stand with your feet shoulder width apart in a comfortable position. The racket and ball should be together, pointing roughly to the target at which you are aiming. It is a good idea to hold only one ball in your hand at a time, as it makes the place-up easier.

The ball and racket head must work rhythmically together throughout the serve. Both arms go down and outwards as the shoulders open up. As the front arm comes upwards, the ball is released, while the racket arm is bending and so dropping the racket onto the back. The racket head is then 'thrown' at the ball.

The ball must be placed at a comfortable height (it is generally best to place it slightly above your reach, and contact the ball just as it falls) and slightly in front and to the racket side of the body.

The ball should be contacted at a full hitting height with a firm but flexible wrist. The racket then follows through in the direction of the ball, ending at the left side of the body (for a right-hander). Try to maintain good balance throughout the stroke and then recover to the ready position.

The ready position for the service. Feet are a comfortable distance apart. The ball and racket start together — pointing at the box to which the server is aiming.

Helpful hints on the serve

a Start the serve in a relaxed manner, with your weight forward, pointing to the box into which you are serving; relax your arms (let them drop).

b In order to place up the ball correctly, hold it in your fingertips.

c Release the ball when your arm is straight.

d Ensure your place-up arm goes out in front of you and not to the side.

e Try not to flick your fingers or wrist as you release the ball.

f If the ball is not placed in the right position, leave it.

g Work on developing a strong throwing action (practise throwing tennis balls overarm).

h Bend your knees, arch your back and put your body into the serve.

i Complete the serve with a good follow-through.

The service in action.
Tim starts in the ready position.

Both arms work rhythmically together. As the racket is taken back, the left arm starts to come upwards and so releases the ball.

The ball is placed high in the air and the racket is taken out at the back.

The racket is about to drop onto the back. Note the knee bend so that the player can use his leg strength to drive up to the ball.

The racket has dropped down onto the back and is about to be thrown up at the ball as the player extends upwards. Note the elbow bend.

The most typical service faults

a Wrong grip (it is very difficult to get controlled speed and spin with a forehand grip).

b Ball placed too high.

c Ball placed too low.

d Ball placed too far behind your head.

e Ball hit after it has dropped too low.

f Lack of a throwing action (the ball is just pushed into play).

g Lack of co-ordination between place-up arm and racket arm.

h Back foot and hip coming round too early, with the result that the ball goes into the net.

The racket is thrown up at the ball. The player in this instance is now off the ground.

Contact with the ball is made at the player's maximum reach.

As the player follows through, he lands inside the court and the racket finishes past the left side of his body.

THE RETURN OF SERVE

If the serve is the most important shot in the game, then the return of serve is the next most important. However, it is probably practised the least. For most people, the only time the return of serve is practised is actually during the course of a game!

Cast your mind back to your last game: did you make all the returns of serve? How many times did the ball sail straight out over the baseline, or drift into the net? Why? Did you tense up because the ball was coming slightly harder than a normal ground stroke? Were you nervous because you thought you had to hit the ball back hard, and so you froze and did not move forwards to the oncoming serve?

Don't worry about trying to hit the cover off the ball: just block it, chip it, or chop it, but *force your opponent* to *hit another ball after the serve*. Your aim is to achieve a consistent return so that your opponent has to do something with the ball. Once the ball is in play, you are in the rally. You must think positively and aggressively, but the action must be like a shortened ground stroke, and must be fairly compact. If you have a large takeback, the chances are that you will contact the ball late and it will end up long or over the sideline.

Where you stand depends on the power of the serve. If your

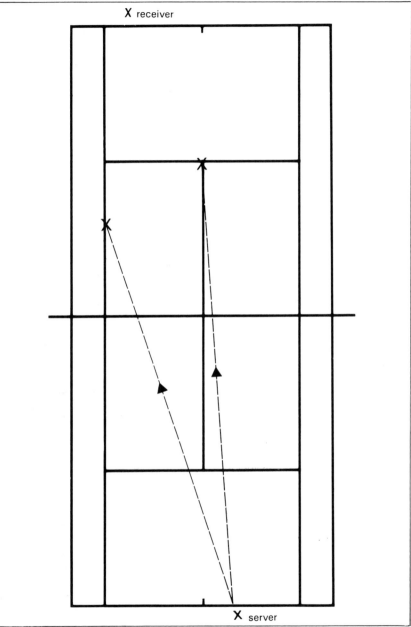

Fig. 5 *Where to stand (X) for the return of serve.*

34

opponent has a weak serve, move in and be aggressive. Conversely, if your opponent has a very powerful serve, you will probably need to stand further back behind the baseline.

As a guideline, stand on or just behind the baseline and a few feet from the singles sideline, but in such a position that you can cover the angles to which the opponent might serve (i.e. you can cover the flat serve down the centre line and the wide slice serve).

Try to tune into the serve early by focusing on the ball once it is in your opponent's hand. Keep watching the ball as it is placed up so that you are prepared for the serve; this will also help you to react earlier. Pick up clues as to where your opponent is going to serve: for example, if the ball is placed over the server's head, it is going to have some topspin on it, as well as some kick, making it bounce to the left. If the ball is placed to the right (generally served to the right court if hit by a right-hander), it will have some slice on it and will stay low on bouncing; if the place-up is high, it will probably be hit hard and flat, so stay back a little; if the server stands very close to the centre line, watch out for the cannon ball down the centre service line. If the server stands wide, be ready for a wide ball.

The return of service.
The returner starts in the ready position just behind the baseline.

As the server places the ball up, the returner starts to move forwards.

35

The key to good returning is to think *early* and to keep moving *forwards*. Have a short takeback and keep the racket behind the ball. If you keep moving forwards on the return, particularly against a sliced serve, you will meet it before it gets too far away from you. One of the best returners in the game is Jimmy Connors, who clearly exemplifies the actions of picking up the ball *early* and moving *forwards* to it. Always make sure that you get your body behind the return of serve.

I can remember one of my pupils saying to his partner at break point in a vital doubles match, 'pick your target and go for it!' He did just that and hit a blistering return down the line. Think positively, and picture where you are going to hit the return.

As the server strikes the ball, the returner 'checks' to get himself balanced.

The returner moves forwards to the ball.

36

The returner is about to step in and strike the ball.

THE VOLLEY

Technically, the volley is the simplest of all the shots in tennis and is certainly the easiest to teach. Volleying can be great fun, and is a vital tool in your tennis armoury if you wish to develop an all-court game. Certainly, if you play doubles it is essential.

For the beginner the easiest grips to use are the basic Eastern forehand on a forehand volley, and the Eastern backhand for the backhand volley. As you progress, you will find it more convenient to use one grip, the chopper grip. This will suffice for both types of volley, so making it easier to hit a succession of forehand and backhand volleys. Net play often involves split second timing, and there is just not enough time to change the grip.

Typical mistakes on the return of serve

a The return goes too long, probably because you are nervous and as a result do not step into the ball. Try finishing with your racket pointing towards the intended target.

b The return either lands short or goes into the net. This generally occurs when there is no lift, so bend your knees and stay low.

c Difficulty in hitting the ball to its intended target is a common fault when the ball is played late, so prepare early and go to meet the ball in front. Also, pick a target and aim for it.

The forehand volley

Start from the ready position. This is now approximately 2.25 metres (6 ft) from the net (touch the net with your racket and take two paces back). As you are now much nearer to your opponent, make sure you start in an alert, 'springy' position. Hold the racket out in front of you and support it at the throat with your free hand. Bend your body over towards the target, and make sure your knees are slightly bent. Keep your eyes fixed on your opponent and the ball, and this will

The forehand volley shadowed.
The ready position for the volley. The racket is held in front of the body and is supported by the free hand.

The racket is taken back with a very short action.

help you to decide to which side the ball is coming.

Prepare early for the volley with a short backswing (no further than the shoulder). Contact the ball out in front of you, at a comfortable distance from your body, and with a slightly bent arm. As you move forwards to the ball, transfer your weight onto your leading foot. *Punch* or *block* the ball, letting the racket do the work, with little follow-through. If the follow-through is too long, you will not have time to get ready for the next volley. Maintain a firm grip when the ball contacts the racket and keep balanced throughout the stroke.

The racket action is a punch *or* block *with little follow-through. The ball is played in front of and to the side of the body.*

Once the shot is completed, recover quickly to the ready position.

If you are a player who uses a Western or semi-Western forehand grip for a volley, you will find it very difficult to hit the low volley. This is an example of when a change of grip is necessary.

Do not forget that it is just as easy to win the point with a well-placed volley as it is with a powerful one. Play the simple percentge shot rather than the flashy powerful one!

The forehand volley in action.
Corinna has a short takeback. Her body weight is about to be transferred forwards.

Typical faults on the forehand volley

a Wrong grip, e.g. semi-Western forehand grip.

b Ball hit behind you.

c Too large a takeback.

d Too large a follow-through.

e Waiting for the ball to reach you, rather than going forwards to meet it.

f Racket is held at a vertical angle to the ground (this is a characteristic of beginners when they volley, with the result that it is difficult to hit the ball to a length).

As the player steps into the shot, the racket comes forwards.

Above, left *The ball is contacted in front of the body with a punch action.*

Above, right *The follow-through is short and in front of the body.*

g Dropping of the racket head.

h Wrist not firm enough on impact.

i Positioning too close to the body.

j Too open a stance.

k Mishitting by not watching the ball carefully enough.

The ball must always be watched carefully to avoid mishitting it.

The one-handed backhand volley shadowed.
The ready position. A chopper grip or backhand grip can be used.

The backhand volley

The backhand volley can be played with either one or two hands. Several players who hit two-handed ground strokes often hit one-handed volleys, and many others are capable of the one-handed volley when stretched wide for a ball.

For the one-handed volley, start from the ready position as mentioned previously. Again, there is a short takeback, but this time the racket is supported with the free hand, which only comes off just before the ball hits the racket strings. As the racket is brought forwards in a *punching* or *blocking*

The racket, supported by the free hand, is taken back. Note the short takeback.

The action is a punch or block *with little follow-through. The body weight is going forwards.*

The two-handed backhand volley in action.
The racket takeback is short.

As the ball approaches, the player steps into the shot and at the same time brings his racket forwards.

action, the ball is contacted well in front of and at a comfortable distance from the body. The arm is slightly bent. To get some power into the shot, transfer your weight onto your front foot. A good volley will have little or no follow-through. Naturally, the grip must be firm on contact, good balance must be maintained throughout the stroke, and a quick recovery must be made to the ready position, as in the forehand volley.

The two-handed backhand volley has the same action, although in most cases the takeback will probably be slightly greater. The hands are positioned next to each other on the grip. The obvious limitation of two hands on the volley is that of reach, which means the volleyer must be quicker on his feet, or alternatively must be able to play a one-handed volley if pulled wide.

The advantage of the two-handed volley is that you will be able to achieve more power and often more dexterity than with a one-handed shot.

The main faults are similar to those on the forehand volley, with the addition of:

a little or no use of the free hand on the takeback

b no power

c lack of shoulder turn

d racket face too open (ball tends to float up into the air).

Above *Contact with the ball is made with a punching or blocking action to the side and in front of the body.*
Above, right *The follow-through is short and in front of the body.*

The low forehand volley.
The ideal position for the low forehand volley. The player has a good knee bend; the racket head is up and the racket face is slightly open.

The low forehand volley in action.

The player starts to move forwards for the volley.

The player begins to bend her knees and gets down to the ball. Note the short takeback of the racket.

The low volley

The volleys discussed so far have been the easy, basic shoulder-height ones, but unfortunately your opponent will not always be kind. He will try to make it as difficult as possible for you at the net, and one of the ways of doing this is for him to hit the ball very low over the net. This is what might aptly be called the 'killer' low volley. How many times have you hit such a shot straight into the bottom of the net?

The low volley is generally played when you are a long way from the net, or when your opponent has hit a devastating return at your feet.

The ball is struck with a good knee bend; the racket face is slightly open and in front of the body.

There are three basic points you need to understand to hit a good, low volley. Firstly, for any ball at net height or below, bend your knees and not your back! This might even mean touching the ground with your knee! Secondly, open the racket face so that it is tilted back slightly, enabling the ball to come up quickly and clear the net.

Right *The ideal position for the low backhand volley. The player really bends down to the ball; the racket head is up and the racket face is slightly open.*

The low backhand volley in action.

The player sees that the oncoming ball is low and so starts to bend her knees and open the racket face slightly.

45

Finally, keep the racket head up, rather than letting it drop onto the ground.

The low volley is played with a short punch, out in front of the body. Acknowledge the fact that you are in trouble if you have to play a low volley, and hit the ball back deep into your opponent's court, making it more difficult for him to pass you. Do not try to hit it too hard, because you are likely either to hit the top of the net or to send the ball straight over the baseline!

Contact with the ball is made in front of the body with a slightly open racket face.

The follow-through is slightly upwards to help lift the ball over the net.

The high volley

If the ball comes to you at a height above your shoulder or head, but not high enough to enable you to smash, you are faced with the high volley. This volley is easy to execute, but all too often the ball goes out of court. Watch the ball carefully, and then set yourself up to play the volley with a high racket takeback. The action is exaggerated, from high to low, and the ball is played well out in front of the body. It is best to hit this volley deep, so let the racket go forwards: do not be drawn into the trap of trying to snap the racket down quickly, otherwise the volley will end up in the net.

The high forehand volley shadowed.

Above, left *The racket head is taken back well above shoulder height.*

Above, centre *The racket then comes down in a high-to-low action, with ball contact at approximately shoulder height.*

Above, right *The follow-through is short.*

The reflex volley

Sometimes you have to cope with a ball which is hit directly at you when you are near the net. The ball is travelling fast, so this is, in reality, a reflex action. It is easiest to accomplish by holding the racket in front of the body in a backhand action, with the racket face parallel to the ground, and then to play the ball in front of the body. It is not uncommon to see a club player duck and get quickly out of the way!

47

The high backhand volley shadowed.
The racket is taken back well above shoulder height and is supported by the free hand.

The racket action is a high-to-low one. The racket face is slightly open to enable the player to put backspin on the ball.

The follow-through is short.

VARIATIONS OF THE VOLLEY

So far, only the basic volley actions have been discussed, but there are several variations on the volley, all of which you can have great fun with on the practice court; once competent with them, you can have a good deal of satisfaction using them at the correct time in matches!

The half-volley

The half-volley is the shot you might be forced to use when coming into the net but not getting there quickly enough, or, alternatively (and this is far more likely), because your opponent has hit a devastating shot at your feet! It is played almost immediately after the ball bounces, at just about ground level. You have probably played it instinctively on several occasions. It is a defensive shot, and is normally

hit when a player is out of position. A half-volley is also a compact shot in which footwork and balance are essential.

One of the most important points to remember when playing the half-volley is to get down to the ball, even if this means putting your knee on the ground. The swing of the racket is from low to high, and the ball must be contacted in front of you. Use a short backswing and extend the follow-through in the direction in which you want the ball to go. The racket face will be slightly open on impact; obviously, if it is too open, the ball will fly over the baseline. Maintain a firm grip and wrist on impact with the ball.

Half-volleys are normally hit down the line. They should be hit deep and low, making it difficult for your opponent to pass you and easier for you to cover the passing shots. If the half-volley is played crosscourt, your opponent will find it easy to pass you down the line. The exception comes when playing doubles, when the half-volley is played crosscourt and not down the line at the net player. If your opponent is coming into the net, the half-volley is played short. Normally, a half-volley played midcourt would provide an easy winner for your opponent.

Main problems with the half-volley

a The ball goes too long, because you stand up too early; to overcome this, bend your knees, stay down low and ensure the ball is hit in front of you.

b The ball lands too short or in the net; this occurs when you do not get below the ball, so try to move down as soon as your opponent hits it. Don't forget: bend your knees and not your back!

The drive volley

The drive volley is sometimes used as an approach shot, and is hit from the midcourt area. As its name suggests, it is both a drive and a volley, and thus has some of the characteristics of both. As for a drive, use a longer backswing than for a normal volley; in order to control the ball, it is also best to hit with a little topspin. It is a difficult shot to control, and is best learned after mastering the basic volley. You have probably unknowingly hit several drive volleys when trying to hit a punched, or blocked, volley!

The tactical uses of the drive volley are against a slow, high ball when close to the net; against high balls when coming to the net; or as an element of surprise by moving quickly off the baseline and not allowing a floating return to bounce.

The drop volley

The drop volley is similar to the drop shot, except that it is played before the ball bounces. It requires a great deal of touch and feel for the ball on the racket strings, and gives you enormous satisfaction when played well. The drop volley is played when the ball is at or below net height.

In order to play the shot, use a short backswing and reduced follow-through. The wrist should be firm, but the racket face open at impact to increase the amount of backspin put on the ball. It is imperative to watch the ball carefully, to keep your head over the ball and to

bend your knees. A good drop volley keeps the ball very short in your opponent's half of the court and, naturally, kills the speed of an attempted passing shot. It can be very effective as an element of surprise when used against an opponent who is standing well behind the baseline. It requires a great deal of practice to master the shot, but it is well worth it when you see the results.

The lob volley

Another variation of the volley is the lob volley, which is probably played more in doubles matches than in singles. It is like the basic lob, but is played before the ball bounces. Use the normal volley grips, with a short backswing and a firm wrist. The racket face is opened on impact to give lift and some degree of backspin; the racket follow-through is upwards, but fairly short. Try to bend your knees.

This is another shot which needs a fine touch and which, if played badly, can have devastating consequences for you – especially if your opponent is in an easy smashing position! Tactically, its function is one of surprise; it can be used when your opponent is very close to the net, and can enable you to open up the court for possible angles. If you can play the lob volley and your opponent knows you possess this shot in your

The drop volley in action.

Above *The preparation and takeback are the same as for an ordinary volley with a short backswing.*

Above, right *On impact the racket face is open, thereby enabling backspin to be imparted onto the ball.*

Right *The racket comes down and under the ball so that on the follow-through the racket face is far more open than on a normal volley. The action is like that of a letter 'C'.*

repertoire, it tends to make him stay back from the net.

A typical mistake when playing the lob volley is to hit the ball too late and not high enough; the racket face is not sufficiently open, so the racket head is under the ball.

THE LOB

The lob is probably one of the shots most underused by the average player and is often looked upon as a 'hacking' shot. However, when used effectively and at the right time, it can be devastating.

The lob is not just a defensive shot, only to be played when you are in trouble – far from it. The topspin attacking lob can easily win the point outright against an aggressive volleyer. The lob is not a sign of weakness, but more often is a sign of intelligent play and a desire to stay in the point.

There are two types of lob: defensive and offensive. A defensive lob is generally hit from behind the baseline, or when you are stretched wide out of court. The aim is to put the ball up high to give yourself time to get back into position.

An offensive lob is hit lower and generally from inside the baseline. The idea is to hit the ball just high enough so that your opponent cannot reach it, but not so high that he has time to turn and chase the ball.

When learning in the early stages how to hit a lob, it is easiest to concentrate on a simple defensive lob.

The forehand lob

This is played in a similar way to the forehand drive, with two

Fig. 6a The forehand lob sequence of shots.

notable exceptions. Starting from the ready position, take the racket back early and then make a smooth connection between the back swing and the forward swing. The swing is from low to high, but the *racket face must be slightly open* on impact with the ball. The follow-through is then *slightly higher* than for a normal forehand. Again, the ball is hit in front of the body and a comfortable distance to the side, and the body weight is transferred forwards.

Fig. 6b The backhand lob sequence of shots.

The lob is very much a touch shot which needs a lot of control. Imagine you are attempting to place the ball on a cloud in the sky, so slow the ball down and try to hit it delicately and softly. Lift the ball gently into the air with your open racket face and high follow-through. If you try to 'blast' the lob, the ball will just end up several feet over the baseline!

The backhand lob

The backhand lob is hit in the same way as the backhand drive, but with an open racket face on impact and a higher follow-through.

Do not be afraid to use the lob as a means of trying to break up your opponent's rhythm. A hard hitter generally dislikes soft 'moon' balls, so throw in the lob to disrupt his pattern of play.

A few useful tips on the lob

a Use a long, smooth stroke, trying to keep the ball on the racket for as long as possible.

b Attempt to get the highest point of the lob directly above or slightly behind your opponent.

c Always try to lob over your opponent's backhand side. A poor lob on the backhand is still a harder

shot to hit than a full-blooded smash.

As soon as you put up a lob, start moving and be prepared to run. If it is a poor lob, you are going to have to chase the smash and scramble the ball back again. If it is a good lob, you should be looking to follow it into the net to put away the return. Whatever happens, be prepared to move.

The topspin lob

There is no greater feeling of satisfaction than that experienced when hitting an effective topspin lob. It is a very difficult shot for your opponent to return, because having whipped the ball up over your opponent's head, it then drops rapidly, but on striking the ground it kicks off towards the baseline, leaving your opponent scrambling to get the ball back again.

It is, however, a difficult shot to hit, and requires a great deal of skill and expertise. You will need to be able to hit a good topspin ground stroke before you can attempt the topspin lob. Unless you can put plenty of spin on the ball, you will find you are putting up an easy lob which can readily be smashed away.

You will find it more difficult to hit a topspin lob on a fast surface than on a slow one, where the ball sits up higher, giving you time to whip up the back of the ball. The ball needs to be contacted with the racket face almost vertical to the ground, and the racket should move in an upward and forward direction. It is necessary to have a firm grip, otherwise you will find yourself mishitting the ball. Uncock your wrist on impact, and have a good follow-through. The point of impact is generally just behind your front foot, and you will probably find the shot easier to hit with an open stance (i.e. facing the net).

Next time you get a few spare minutes on the practice court, experiment with some topspin lobs. It requires a lot of feel for the ball on the racket, but it is a great shot to play.

Typical mistakes on the lob

a Wrong grip.

b Not enough height on the ball (racket face is not open enough, knees not bent enough).

c Lob too long (you could be overhitting).

d Swing too big (shorten takeback).

e Lob too short (aim for the baseline).

f Lack of direction (check area of contact and angle of racket face).

THE SMASH

When you are at the net you are going to have to play either a volley or a smash – or you might have to run like the wind and chase the topspin lob! If you can develop a good overhead, you can be devastating at the net. Immense satisfaction can be gained from cracking an overhead for an outright winner. If you enjoy smashing, you will welcome the lob!

Many average players dread the smash, generally because they make so many mistakes with it. It is easy to detect a person who hates smashing because of the way he prepares for the shot: he fiddles and fusses around, his feet are all over the place and he has no balance – it is small wonder he misses a high percentage of smashes! It is well worth spending time on developing your overhead, and one of the keys to success will be your footwork.

In many ways the smash is very much like the serve, but it ought to be easier because you do not have to worry about putting the ball up in the air, as your opponent will do that for you. However, you do need a good pair of legs, because you must run and get under the ball. Good smashers have good footwork, and really reach up and go for the ball.

The smash differs from the serve because it has a much shorter takeback. Instead of the racket extending right out at the back of the body, it is just taken straight behind your shoulder into the 'back scratching' position. This is necessary, as the smash requires

more precise timing, and the ball on the smash is falling from a greater height than on the service place-up.

Start from the ready position at the net, with your chopper grip (beginners may initially use a forehand grip). As soon as you see your opponent open his racket face, lean backwards or start an abbreviated swing — all clues that he is going to put up a lob — begin to prepare by taking the racket straight onto your back.

The key to the smash lies in moving as quickly as possible to a position underneath the ball. Ideally, you should get so far back that you can move onto the ball. Like the service, the ball should be hit in front and slightly to the right of the body (if right-handed).

Do not forget: your opponent is going to make it as hard as possible for you to position yourself, so you will really have to move. When you are underneath the ball, try to be in a sideways position, again as in the serve. If you smash facing the net, all too often the ball ends up in the bottom of the net — something many of us have experienced!

Once in the sideways position and under the ball, really throw the racket head up to the ball. Pick a target and go for it; do not hit the ball gently back into court. This is the moment you have been waiting for — kill the ball and get your

body weight behind the shot. To help you sight the ball and maintain good balance, point your free hand up at the ball, but do watch the ball and not your hand!

The player is positioned and waiting to hit the smash. Notice the sideways stance, the racket behind the head, the player pointing up at the ball for balance and the eyes focused on the ball.

The smash in action.
Corinna starts to prepare for the smash with a shortened backswing.

Make sure you follow through in the direction of the ball and then recover to the ready position. Do not just stand there and admire your smash, but prepare for the next shot – you'll be surprised how this will help your follow-through. When retreating for the smash, run back in a sideways movement – it is far easier to get to the ball!

Not all smashes are the same. Sometimes the lobbed ball is so high that it is easier to smash it after the bounce; on a windy or very sunny day, it might be a

The racket is now on her back and she points with her left hand up at the ball.

The point of contact with the ball is at the player's maximum reach.

Like the service action, the follow-through is down past the left side of the body.

tactical ploy to let the ball bounce, unless you are extremely confident about hitting the ball in the air. Even hitting a smash after the bounce can be difficult, but again it depends on your footwork. You must position yourself underneath and behind the ball. The ball will not bounce up vertically, so stand a little further back, and if necessary then move forwards to the ball. Likewise, if a shallow lob is put up, move quickly onto the ball before it gets too low and you end up hitting it over the baseline.

As you become more experienced and more confident with the smash try 'jumping' for the ball. Your ability to leap for the ball will make it even more difficult for your opponent to get the ball out of your reach. The key to success is to co-ordinate the jump with the throwing action. As you take the racket back, start to jump, and complete the throwing action and jump at the same time. It is simplest if you take off on one foot and land on the other.

There is also a backhand smash, but this is far more difficult to play, and if at all possible run round the ball to play the forehand smash (again, this necessitates good and quick footwork). Obviously it is harder to generate a lot of power on the backhand smash, so you should attempt to be accurate with the hit. You need really to turn the right shoulder (if you are right-handed)

around behind the ball to give you the chance of throwing the racket down and through the ball.

Above all, be decisive on the smash. Go for the winner. It might need a lot of practice, but think of all the satisfaction when you get it right.

Typical mistakes on the smash

a Wrong grip (chopper grip should be used once a basic throwing action is established).

b Smash too long – generally when the ball is hit behind you.

c Poor footwork, and not getting back quick enough.

d Smash into net (try to get into a sideways position).

e Not watching the ball.

f Poor throwing action.

g Poor balance.

h Little use of the free arm.

THE DROP SHOT

The drop shot is perhaps one of the most underused shots at junior and club level, but when played at the correct time it can be immensely valuable. The aim is to get the ball to land as near to the net as possible; if sufficient spin is put on the ball, it will actually die as it hits the ground, or even bounce back towards the net. On a windy day it is possible for the ball to rebound back over the net, but you need a great deal of touch and skill to do this! For the average player, though, it is worth just concentrating on trying to get the ball to land as

near to the net as possible. The drop shot can be played from anywhere on the court, but the further back it is played, the more risky the shot becomes, and the greater the margin for error. Unless you possess good touch, practise the drop shot from an offensive position, when the ball lands in or around the service box. The key to a good drop shot is deception.

Generally, the drop shot is used for strategic reasons: for example, when playing a baseliner, a drop shot will force the player to come to the net. Listed below are some examples of when a drop shot can be used to good effect:

a to tire your opponent; this tactic could be used at the start of and fairly frequently during a match

b to break up your opponent's rhythm

c when trying to bring a poor volleyer to the net

d when wishing to surprise an opponent

e when playing against an opponent who is slow around the court or is physically out of condition

f as a surprise element against a weak second serve

g as a reply to another drop shot

h when playing against the wind

i when your opponent is standing very deep, and he returns a shot which lands near the service box.

The forehand dropshot shadowed.

Above, left *The player begins in the ready position.*

Above, centre *The racket is taken back at approximately shoulder height and the player starts to move towards the ball.*

Above, right *The racket then comes down and under the ball with an open racket face.*

Left *On impact, the racket face is open.*

Right *The follow-through is slightly upward. The whole action is similar to that of a letter 'C'.*

There are also certain situations when it is inadvisable to play a drop shot:

a when you are hitting with the wind, because the ball will be taken forwards and will be too easy to return

b when you are in a defensive position

c when you are standing behind the baseline or deep in court

d on important points, e.g. 15–30, 30–40, because it is too risky

e when playing a quick opponent, particularly on hard surfaces where the bounce is generally higher than on other surfaces

f if you are returning a high-bouncing ball

g if your opponent has hit the ball very hard

h when the ball is played down the centre of the court.

One of the most important things to remember is only to play the drop shot when you are *moving forwards* to the ball, not when you are stationary or moving laterally.

Playing the drop shot

A good drop shot must be disguised, i.e. made to look like your normal forehand or backhand drive. Prepare normally, with the racket takeback and head above the level at which you intend to hit the ball. The racket then comes down in a 'C' shape; at the point of impact it is slightly open, and the

follow-through is under the ball, so imparting backspin on it. The ball is kept on the racket for as long as possible. A firm grip is required. If hit correctly, the drop shot will float through the air, clear the net and land close to it, causing your opponent to run very quickly to retrieve the ball. It is necessary to

The backhand dropshot shadowed.
The racket takeback is high and the racket is supported with the free hand.

have a good follow-through in the direction in which you want the ball to go.

In the early stages of learning to play a drop shot, let the ball clear the net by a reasonable margin, e.g. three or four feet, and work on imparting spin on the ball, rather than trying to hit a drop shot which

The player steps into the shot.

58

just skims the net. It takes a lot of experience and practice to perfect a good drop shot.

The simplest drop shot to play is one down the line, because the ball has the least distance to travel; the shorter the distance, the easier it is to judge the speed that must be put onto the stroke. However, in the case of a beginner, it might be better for the drop shot to be played crosscourt (when a greater distance is involved); even if it is not well executed, at least the ball is travelling over the side line and will therefore take the opponent out of court. If a poor drop shot is played straight and sits up, it could readily be hit away for a winner.

If you are faced with the prospect of countering a drop shot, there are two easy solutions.

a Return the ball with another drop shot. This is often effective at a low level of play, because your opponent stands and admires his

The racket comes down and under the ball with an open racket face.

The follow-through is slightly upward. The whole action is similar to that of a letter 'C'.

The backhand dropshot in action.
The racket takeback is high.

Contact with the ball is made with an open racket face.

drop shot, assuming he has hit a winner!

b A good reply is to hit the ball deep down the line and as low as possible, making it difficult for your opponent to pass you.

Do remember that it is difficult to hit a drop shot for an outright winner, but that often the drop shot can be used to set up a situation for you to hit the next ball for a winner.

Have some fun trying to develop your touch on the drop shot, but think carefully about the best surface for playing this shot. Grass courts and clay courts are ideal, but on high-bouncing hard courts, even good drop shots tend to sit up, and can be easily chased down.

The follow-through is out in front of the body. Some players may find it easier with very little follow-through.

5 SPIN

USE OF SPIN ON THE GROUND STROKES

Once you have mastered the basics of the forehand and backhand drives, you will need to vary these shots. Ways of doing this are to spin a ball, to make the ball kick up high when playing with people who dislike a shoulder-height ball, or to make the ball skid low for tall people who are not very good at bending their knees. You need to have an understanding of ball rotation in order to hit with spin, so that you can change the pace of the game and upset your opponent's rhythm.

As soon as he can hit a few balls over the net, the average youngster wants to learn how to hit with topspin like the stars. Topspin is not the only spin that can be put on a ball; there is also sidespin (or slice) and underspin (or chip).

With topspin the ball spins from low to high on a vertical axis. This causes a downward force, and the path of the ball is like the arch of a rainbow.

Sidespin refers to a ball revolving in a horizontal plane, generating a curving ball to your left or right, and so moving away from your opponent. It is mostly used on the serve.

Underspin, or slice, is played with the racket path going from high to

The topspin forehand is played with a closed racket face.

The topspin forehand.
The racket head comes from below the ball.

The ball is struck in a low-to-high swing, with the racket travelling vertically up the back of the ball and so imparting spin onto it.

low; it generates an upward force until gravity takes over, so that the ball tracks in the line of an inverted rainbow arch, and is thus opposite to topspin.

Topspin

Topspin is easier to learn and control than slice, particularly for the beginner. Topspin is more reliable under pressure; it is safer and leads to a stronger, all-court game. You can hit the ball hard with topspin, but safely over the net by four to six feet (1.2–1.8 metres) as the spin imparted will bring the

ball down. If you hit a flat ball very hard and deep, it has to be hit lower over the net to keep the ball in play, thus giving little margin for error.

The use of topspin on the ground strokes increased markedly after the successes of Bjorn Borg at the end of the 1970s. Borg used excessive topspin on both sides. Clay courts suit the use of topspin with their slow, high bounce, and, as many tournaments are played on clay, it is only sensible to be able to hit with topspin.

Start from the ready position. Prepare as for a normal drive and then bring the racket down lower (i.e. drop your racket head down below your waist, at least 30 cm (12 in) below the intended point of impact). The racket face is then slightly closed, and the ball is struck in a low to high swing, with the racket head approaching a vertical position to the ground on impact. The more spin you want to generate, the more the racket head will approach this position; hit from 6 to 12 o'clock.

The follow-through is long, smooth and high.

***The topspin backhand** is played with a closed racket face.*

The follow-through is up and over the ball.

Follow through over the ball with a long, smooth, high finish in the direction of your target. Hit the ball out in front, so your body weight goes into the shot. Often you need to bend your knees to get your racket head and wrist lower and below the ball.

The grip most suited to heavy topspin is the Western or semi-Western forehand grip. You might find it easier to hit the ball in a semi-open stance.

The topspin backhand is played in a similar fashion to the forehand.

From the ready position, change the grip to an Eastern backhand and turn early at the shoulders. Again, the racket head is then taken well below the ball, being supported with your free hand to give you more control and make you aware of the racket face. Transfer your body weight onto the front foot as you prepare to make contact with the ball. Bring the racket head vertically up the back of the ball and forwards. Accelerate the racket head through the stroke to achieve momentum and power.

Follow through high and in the direction of the target. The ball should be contacted in front of you. If you play a single-handed backhand you might find this shot harder to master than your double-handed counterpart, and it will require a lot of practice.

If you are double-handed it is easier and sounder to use an Eastern backhand grip; you might even release your supporting hand on the long follow-through, as some professionals do.

There are two myths about hitting

topspin which often cause confusion. Firstly, it is not necessary to use the wrist to roll the racket *over the ball* at impact to impart topspin. Certainly, many good players use their wrist when hitting topspin, but on impact it is firm, and it rolls over after impact. Secondly, you do not require a lot of strength to hit powerful topspin, and you only need a strong wrist when you hit the ball late and want a sudden burst of racket head speed. It is important to get into position early and then to co-ordinate the body and racket arm as the ball is struck; you will then be able to hit it hard.

Uses of topspin

a To give yourself a good margin for error when hitting the ball hard and deep.

b It produces a high bounce, giving your opponent a difficult shot to play.

The topspin backhand in action.
As the ball approaches, the player turns and takes the racket back.

The racket head then comes below the ball.

The racket face is slightly closed on impact.

c Variation to mix up your opponent's game; if he likes a hard, low ball, use a loopy topspin.

d As a passing shot; the ball is hit lower over the net than when playing a normal drive, and will dip down after clearing the net, making the volley more difficult to return.

Typical faults on topspin drives

a Angle of racket face is wrong on impact (if too closed, the ball ends in the bottom of the net).

b Racket head is not far enough below the ball.

c Preparation too late, so ball is contacted late.

d Wrong grip.

e Stance too closed.

The racket brushes up the back of the ball, so imparting spin on the ball.

The follow-through is long and high.

Slice

Slice can be used both as a defensive and an offensive shot, and played effectively it can be devastating. Slice is used defensively from the baseline, often because a player has not moved into a good hitting position. It can also be used to good effect to change the direction and pace of the ball.

Offensively, the slice is played as an approach shot, when an opponent has hit a short ball and the other player wants to come in to the net. The ball has a lower trajectory than topspin, will thus stay low on bouncing, and so will force the opponent to lift the ball to get it over the net. If you are coming into the net, this then gives you a rising ball to volley.

The slice forehand is generally only used as an approach shot against a high bouncing ball, although it can be played as a last resort when you do not have time to drive the ball. From the ready position, turn your shoulder as the ball approaches you, and take the racket back above the level of the ball. The racket head is above the firm wrist. Transfer your weight forwards and contact the ball out in front of you, with a slightly open racket face. Keep the follow-through short and in the direction of the target. Obviously this shot is extremely difficult to execute with a Western grip!

The slice backhand is more widely played than the forehand, and is easy to use as an approach shot. Its neat, compact swing naturally makes you lean into the shot. From the ready position, change the grip to a full Eastern backhand and, as the ball approaches, turn your shoulder, while taking the racket head back above the level of the ball.

With a firm wrist, bite into the ball with a high to low swing, and the

The slice backhand shadowed.

As the player turns at the hips and shoulders, the racket head is taken back high.

The racket comes down in a high-to-low swing.

racket face slightly open. The contact point is in front of the body. The follow-through should be smooth, but not too long. If used as an approach shot, let the momentum of the shot and follow-through carry you on into the net.

Many players who hit two-handed backhand drives find it hard to slice with two hands, because the supporting arm restricts the follow-through and it does not flow as a natural shot. They tend to slice with one hand when approaching the net, or in some cases start with two hands on the racket and let the supporting hand come off on the follow-through. Many of the most successful two-handed Swedes, such as Mats Wilander, play a one-handed slice.

Contact with the ball is made in front of the body, with the racket face slightly open.

The follow-through is in front of the body.

The slice backhand in action.
The racket is taken back above shoulder height.

As the player starts the high-to-low swing, the racket face is slightly open.

At the point of impact with the ball, the racket face is open. Note how the player is leaning into the shot.

Typical faults on the slice

a Racket head does not go back above the level of the ball.

b Angle of racket face is wrong on impact: if it is too open, the ball goes too high in the air; if it is too closed, the ball ends up in the bottom of the net!

c Ball hit too late.

d Too much movement while in the sideways position.

USE OF SPIN ON THE SERVE

In tennis there are three types of serve: the flat, the slice, and the topspin (or kick). Remember one

The racket follow-through is out in front of the body.

thing: if you can hold your service throughout the match, each set is going to end up as a tie-break, or there will be a very long last set! It is far more important to develop consistency than power on your serve. You need to be able to get a high percentage of first serves into court so that you are not relying heavily on your second serve and putting extra pressure on yourself.

Let us take a closer look at the spin on the serve, or rather the angle at which the racket strikes the ball, and the degree of ball rotation. On the flat serve the racket contacts the back side of the ball and goes forwards and slightly to the right of the target direction. On the slice serve the racket moves horizontally left to right, brushing round the side of the ball, while on the topspin serve the ball is contacted more in a left to right action (if right-handed) with the racket moving midway between a full vertical and a horizontal plane.

The flat serve

In reality nobody hits an absolutely flat serve, because it is impossible to hit the ball without some form of rotation. However, the so-called flat serve is hit with the least amount of ball rotation. Beginners can use an Eastern forehand grip, but if you want to hit the ball harder and to control it, then you must learn to use the chopper grip. The flat serve is generally hit down

the centre line where the net is lowest and the distance the ball has to travel is the shortest. It is a low-percentage serve, so use it sparingly. A good time to play it is when you are 30–0, 40–0, or 40–15 up, but not when you are break point down and you need to put the first serve into court!

The slice serve

This is played in the same way as the flat serve, except that the racket comes round the side of the ball. A right-hander serving from the right (deuce) court can make the ball break off to his opponent's right, and so take him out of court and force a weak return. The slice serve has a lower trajectory than the flat serve, with the effect that the ball bounces lower. It is therefore very effective against a tall player who hates bending for low balls or moving laterally.

You can readily impart spin on the ball by slightly altering the grip and place-up. If you are right-handed, place the ball further to your right so that you can brush round the side of the ball on contact. You might also find that a slight adjustment of the grip towards an Eastern backhand will enable you to impart more spin on the ball. Many professional players serve with a backhand grip.

Use the natural spin that your body generates when you twist it for the throwing action. You will find that

the contact point is not quite as far in front of you as it would be on the flat service. Your wrist should be fairly loose so that you get a natural snap on impact, and follow through in the usual way.

Most left-handers, e.g. John McEnroe, Martina Navratilova, have a good, natural slice serve. Right-handers can have an equally effective slice serve if they work at it. The reason the left-hander's slice serve is more pronounced is that from an early age a left-hander, who primarily plays against right-handers, discovers that with a bit of slice he can hit the ball to his opponent's backhand and take him well out of court. He therefore often starts working on his slice at an earlier age than a right-hander does. Conversely, the right-hander playing against a right-hander will be serving to his opponent's forehand all the time.

A right-hander serving to another right-hander should only be thinking of using the wide slice serve to the right-hand court when:

a he knows his opponent has a weaker forehand than backhand

b he knows he can ace his opponent

c he knows his opponent has difficulty moving laterally and hitting low balls

d he is sure he will take his opponent out of court.

A slice serve can also be very

effective when used to swing the ball into the opponent's body.

The topspin serve

This is the safest serve of all, and hence its use as a second serve. You must have a proper service grip, as it is impossible to hit this type of serve with a forehand grip.

The place-up for the serve is slightly behind you, so you must sink down, bend your knees and lean back. The racket head comes from low to high, brushing up the back side of the ball, or for a right-hander, from left to right. You might visualise striking the ball from 7 o'clock to 2 o'clock on an imaginary clock. The service grip will give you greater flexibility at the wrist, and also ensures the racket face will be at the right angle for ball rotation. Try to spring up and out at the ball, and get the feeling of hitting up and out. The spin will bring the ball down into your opponent's service box. If hit well, the ball will kick up and outwards, making it difficult for your opponent to return it, particularly on the backhand side.

How to vary the serve

A good serve is a combination of speed, spin and direction. Avoid stereotyping your service, and vary it so that the receiver is kept guessing. Remember the three choices of direction: wide to the corner of the service box; straight down the centre line; and into the body of your opponent. Combine this with the different spins of flat, slice and topspin. Do not forget: your serve requires depth, placement and an element of surprise.

The slice serve is very useful on low bouncing courts, e.g. carpet, supreme, grass or slow red clay. If the grass is slightly damp, the sliced ball will stay very low and may even skid. The short angled slice serve is also very effective on grass. A right-handed player tends to slice the ball wide from the right court and slice it down the centre line from the left court; a left-hander does the opposite. Slice can be used for a first or second serve.

The topspin, or kick serve, is very effective on high bouncing courts, e.g. cement or fast clay. A really hard flat serve on such surfaces is not very successful because the court surface automatically diminishes the power. The kick serve will cause problems, as it is very difficult for your opponent to generate pace from it. You can obviously use this serve on other surfaces as well, as a surprise element, and particularly as a second serve because of its greater margin for error.

The flat serve is effective on a fast surface, but as mentioned previously, it does not allow much room for a mistake. If you possess a hard, flat serve, use it intelligently and wisely.

Do not forget that it is vital to get a high percentage of first serves into play. If you rely too heavily on your second serve you will be putting extra pressure on yourself and you may start to become defensive. As the saying goes, 'You are only as good as your second serve!'

The second serve should always be hit with spin and, in fact, more spin than the first serve. You will need to accelerate the racket head at the ball to impart the spin, so do not 'chicken out' and slow the action down simply because it is a second serve. Always hit the second serve high over the net and deep into the service box, and generally to your opponent's weaker side (in most cases at a lower level to the backhand).

Your second serve will improve with practice. Try to practise it regularly. Always remember that the serve is the most important shot in the game.

6 HOW TO RECOGNISE FAULTS AND CORRECT THEM

Most tennis players, with a little thought and advice from a knowledgeable observer or expert, preferably a coach, can very quickly remedy some of their basic problems. As your standard improves, your game may only need a very minor adjustment, and in this case consult the expert straight away.

The aim of this section is to highlight some of the more common basic errors so that you can have the opportunity of trying to help yourself. Firstly, let's take a look at the *drive*. Are you the type of player who dreads the ball coming onto your backhand? Let's discover what happens to your backhand.

THE BACKHAND DRIVE

Problem	Possible reason(s)	Solution
1. Drive always goes high in the air.	Grip.	Make sure you have the correct grip (see page 13).
	Angle of racket face is too open on impact.	Racket face needs to be more edgeways to the ground on impact.
2. Drive goes into net.	Angle of racket face is too closed. Uncontrolled wrist action. Not enough margin for error.	Try to get more lift on the ball and keep racket face edgeways to ground on impact.
3. Shot is too long.	Racket face too open.	Correct racket face on impact.
	Ball played off backfoot.	Lean into shot.
	Grip.	Check grip.
	Hitting too hard.	More control of racket swing needed.
4. Drive continually going into tramlines.	Too close to the ball. Ball hit too late.	Try to hit at a comfortable distance from the ball. Contact area to be slightly in front of the body.

Perhaps the three most common errors by the average player are as follows.

1. Poor preparation: as soon as the ball leaves your opponent's racket and you know to which side the ball is coming, start to take your racket back. Prepare early.

2. Getting too close to the ball: every shot should be played at a comfortable distance from the body.

3. Using too much wrist on the shot, e.g. turning the wrist over too early causes the ball to end up in the net.

Similar problems arise on the *forehand drive*, with the ball ending up in the net or over the baseline. Again, remember to give yourself comfortable hitting distance, and contact the ball in front of you.

THE SERVICE

Problem	Possible reason(s)	Solution
1. Unable to get any power or speed on the ball.	'Pushing' the racket at the ball. Throwing action poor.	Practise basic throwing action, initially by throwing balls, progressing to racket throwing action and then devoloping racket head speed.
	Ball placement is poor and not in front of the body.	Practise place-ups without hitting the ball.
2. Unable to place the ball in the air correctly.	Flicking of the wrist.	Try to place the ball in the air with a locked wrist.
	Ball released too early (so goes too far forwards).	Release ball when arm is outstretched.
	Jerky action with a bent elbow.	Keep a smooth action and arm straight.
	Ball held too firmly in palm of hand.	Hold ball in finger tips and release by just opening fingers.
Ball over head or too far to the right.	Place-up arm does not go in front of the body.	Let place-up arm go forwards instead of to the side.
3. Unable to hit the ball at your maximum height, even when the ball is placed correctly.	Ball is dropping too low before it is hit.	Hit the ball while it is 'stationary' in the air at the top of its placement.
4. Serve continuously going into net.	Not throwing the racket head at the ball.	Hit up at the ball more. Aim higher over the net.
	Rear foot comes up too early (i.e. hip coming round too early), losing stability and balance for a strong throwing action.	Hold the rear foot on the ground longer (until the ball is struck).

Problem	Possible reason(s)	Solution
5. Service going too long.	Placement of ball too far back.	Place ball in front of body.
	Grip.	If a forehand grip is used, you tend to get underneath the ball.
	Not enough wrist snap.	Snap wrist more after impact, to bring the ball down.
6. Failure to get serve into box when using a chopper grip in the initial stages.	Racket face is not square to the ball and as a result ball is sliced out to the side.	Practise shadow serves into stop netting. Bring shoulder round more on serve or turn wrist slightly.

THE VOLLEY

How many times do you curse yourself when you hit an easy volley straight over the baseline or perhaps the 'sitter' into the bottom of the net? Technically, the volley is the easiest shot to learn, but it is still easy to make mistakes!

Problem	Possible reason(s)	Solution
1. Easy shoulder-height volley is hit out of court.	Racket face is open; often occurs when the backswing is too big. The racket hand is ahead of the racket face.	Do not take the racket back too far. Ensure you punch with the racket face. Hold the racket firmly on impact. Point racket face towards target area. Bend knees more.
2. Low volley consistently going into the net.	Not enough knee bend and getting down to the ball. Racket head is too low. Incorrect angle of racket face.	Keep racket head up more. Racket face needs to be slightly open on impact.
	Grip – especially if a Western grip is used on the forehand side.	Use a chopper grip.
3. Failure to get much power into the volley.	Poor punching action.	Punch or block the ball in front of you. Try to transfer your weight onto your front foot as you volley.
	Playing a late ball.	Try to contact the ball to the side of the body, but well out in front of you.

THE LOB

The lob is probably one of the more underused shots, yet when played effectively and at the right time it can be devastating.

Problem	Possible reason(s)	Solution
1. Not enough height over opponent.	Swing is too shallow.	Try to swing more from low to high with a slightly more open racket face.
	Lifting your head.	Make sure you watch the ball and not your opponent.
	Shortening of swing.	Ensure you have a high follow-through.
2. Mishitting the ball.	Not watching the ball onto the racket.	Watch the ball, rather than your opponent.
	Jerky swing.	Ensure a smooth, slow, low to high swing.
	Playing the ball late.	Try to play the ball in front of the body, in similar fashion to playing ground strokes.
3. Lack of direction on the lob.	Poor follow-through.	Let the racket finish in the direction you want the ball to go (*hint:* try to lob over your opponent's backhand side).

THE SMASH

Do you dread the ball coming over your head when you get to the net? If you do, you are in 'good' company because there are many people who have similar fears. To combat the problem, it is worth spending time on trying to develop a good overhead shot or smash.

It is easy to tell when the average player fears the smash because of the way he prepares for the shot — his feet are all over the place, he has little balance and he doesn't really know what to do.

Problem	Possible reason(s)	Solution
1. Smash always ends up in the net.	Poor positioning of feet, and body is often facing the net prior to impact.	Try to stand sideways onto the net.
	Ball has dropped too low before impact.	Reach up for the ball on the smash.

Problem	Possible reason(s)	Solution
2. Ball ends up long and over baseline.	Poor positioning of feet and body, with result that ball is contacted behind the head.	Try to get far enough back so that you are underneath the ball. Contact ball in front of body. More wrist snap needed.
3. No power in the smash.	Poor throwing action – tendency to push ball back.	Try to develop a proper throwing action.
4. Loss of control when trying to hit to a specific target.	Poor body position. Lack of balance.	Try to get underneath ball more. Point at ball with non-hitting hand to aid balance.

The smash is probably the most enjoyable shot to hit in tennis, especially when you manage to put the ball away for a winner, so try to correct those faults.

THE DROP SHOT

The drop shot requires a lot of practice and feel for the ball on the racket strings ('touch'). A badly hit drop shot can often turn a good strategic position into a hopeless defensive situation, as your opponent pounces on the ball.

Problem	Possible reason(s)	Solution
1. Ball lands too deep in the court.	Not enough backspin on the ball.	Bring the racket under the ball more to impart extra spin. Attack the ball more.
2. Ball passes too high over the net.	Racket face is too open on impact.	Alter angle of the racket face on impact.
3. Ball does not cross the net.	Attempting to put too much spin on the ball.	Try not to come under the ball too much.
4. Lack of touch.	Swing forward too forceful.	Try to get the feeling of cradling the ball on the racket strings.
	Wrist too stiff at the beginning of the stroke.	Relax the wrist more.

It takes experience to perfect this shot, so try to incorporate it into your practice drills.

7 HOW TO PRACTISE

Tennis is a highly skilled game which requires continuous practice if a player's potential is to be fulfilled. For the casual player, practice involves hitting balls up and down the middle of the court, followed by a few volleys, the odd smash, a couple of serves and then a game. However, such an approach neglects probably the best way of self-improvement, i.e. that of practising disciplined drills. This does not mean to say that practice is boring – far from it; constructive practice can be great fun, and provides the opportunity for a tremendous workout.

Drilling is the key to stroke improvement, and is essential in the development of any tennis player. Tennis is a game in which improvement is made through constant repetition, and there is no better way to do this than by drilling. You can focus on one or more aspects of match play in a controlled situation where you are free from the pressures of competition. By repetition of one or more shots, a player can readily 'groove in' his strokes. Every tennis player knows his own concentration span and capacity for drilling, so practice sessions will vary from one individual to another.

This book only gives you a selection of drills and a few ideas about how to practise them. For the more serious player, I would recommend buying a book specifically on tennis drills.

A typical practice session will last approximately one hour. This time period should be divided into sections to allow for:

a warm-up
b practice of main theme
c main theme in a pressurised situation
d conditioned match play using theme
e unconditioned match play
f cool-down.

WARM-UP

During physical training, the body will have to work hard to adapt to the higher levels of stress, so it is advisable to warm up prior to a practice session. There are three main reasons for warming up:

a to protect yourself against injury
b to improve the body's efficiency
c to practise and improve performance (although a warm-up does not actually improve the skills, it can assist in a good performance).

Every player will have his own specific warm-up exercises, but an example of a general routine would be: jogging round the court twice (including sidestepping, lengthening the stride, high knee-raises, etc.), followed by stretching exercises. The stretching should incorporate exercises for the neck, arms, shoulders and chest, back, trunk, buttocks and hips, hamstrings, calf, quadriceps (thighs), groin and ankles.

Always make sure the whole body is warmed up, and relate the warm-up to the activities to be performed.

PRACTICE OF MAIN THEME

An example is the deep crosscourt forehand drive. The two players hit crosscourt forehands to each other. As the players want to practise deep drives, targets can be placed on the court. Players rally for five minutes and count the number of times they hit the target in that time span. For lower level players, the targets should be quite big to ensure a large degree of success. As the standard of the players rises, the targets should become smaller, e.g. ball cans can be used.

MAIN THEME IN A PRESSURISED SITUATION

Players A and B may be very good at hitting deep crosscourt forehands from a static position, but may be prone to error when they have to run for a wide ball. The above drill could therefore be extended by having both players return to the centre mark after each shot (see Fig. 7).

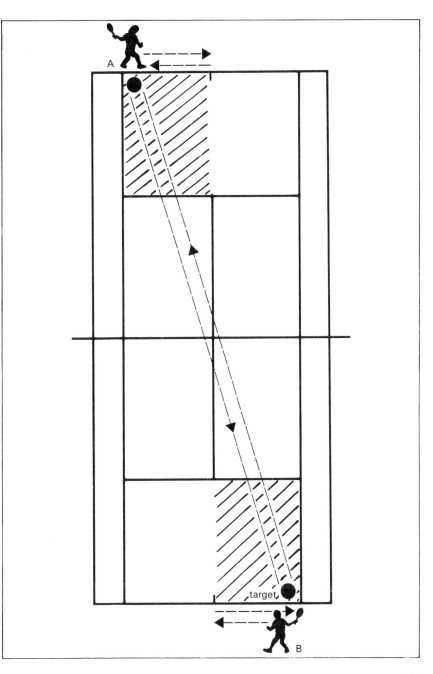

Fig. 7 Crosscourt drives under pressure. Players A and B are rallying crosscourt to the targets. After each shot, they return to the centre mark and so hit groundstrokes on the run.

CONDITIONED MATCH PLAY USING THEME

Points could be played in half of the court only (see the shaded area in Fig. 7), with every ball having to land beyond the service line.

UNCONDITIONED MATCH PLAY

Points or games are played without conditions, but the deep crosscourt forehand drive should now be less prone to breaking down!

COOL-DOWN

It is just as important to cool down after exercise as it is to warm up prior to practising. If the muscles are moved continually in a gentle and rhythmic way, until the body returns to its near-resting state, this will help to prevent stiffness.

Practice can be great fun, and can be done at three different speeds. Consider the deep crosscourt forehand practice.

1. Slow or first gear – this is when the players are standing fairly statically hitting balls to each other. Everything is quite slow and perfectly under control. There is little movement, so the players do not really become very sweaty. This type of practice often occurs when a player is a little tired and lethargic but, even so, the actual skill production of the stroke can be worked on.

2. Medium or second gear – this is the situation in which the players hit crosscourt forehands, for example, and move back to the centre mark after each shot. This gives a good workout if done for 4/5 minutes, particularly if the ball is kept going. Players need to be self-motivated, and push themselves to get back to the middle of the court.

3. Fast or top gear – this is done over a shorter period, but the players go 'flat out'. Player A stands at the net with a basket of balls (25 plus), and feeds continuous balls to B's forehand. The pace and spin on the feeds can be varied. After each shot, player B must try to return to the centre of the court. If this practice is continued for too long, the skill will break down, at which point the practice is no longer beneficial.

This is an ideal practice pressure situation where one player is feeding balls from a basket at the net to another player's forehand. After each shot, the latter returns to the centre mark.

PRACTICE PARTNERS

Finding a practice partner who is better than or equal to you in ability can often cause problems, but this does *not* have to be the case.

You can often have a very good workout practising with somebody who is far worse than you by utilising co-operation drills. Imagine you want to improve your backhand drive. Your partner stands at the net and feeds hundreds of balls to your backhand side. The balls could be fed individually and the pace and depth varied. If your partner is not very good at hitting balls, he can readily hand feed the balls from the net. With controlled, sensible feeding, you could obtain a great deal of benefit from this practice.

When practising with a friend, it is a good idea to try to help each other. Your partner will do something to benefit your game, e.g. hitting balls specifically to your backhand, and then you, in turn, help him, e.g. with the high volley. Here there must be co-operation with the practice partner.

Obviously, the ideal practice partner is somebody who is slightly better than you, who can put the ball in the right place at the right time, push you hard in match play and generally take the game to you, but do not neglect slightly less able players, parents, and friends who could help you.

Another highly successful practice partner is the good old brick wall — at least that doesn't give up or become moody! Alternatively, there is the ball machine, and today there are some highly sophisticated ones which can feed a variety of shots with different spins.

Two county players practising in a co-operation situation. Corinna is practising her volleys, while Tim is working on his groundstrokes.

8 PREPARING FOR COMPETITION

In order to progress in tennis, it is essential to be able to compete, and this involves playing in tournaments. With more people being introduced to tennis via short tennis and 'grass roots coaching courses', there is a demand for numerous tournaments for all ages from six upwards, and for players of different ability levels.

The tournament scene is being re-structured to include many more starter competitions, more one-day tournaments and two-/three-day events, in addition to the highly successful ratings events. This will mean more competitions in which players will be able to compete against opponents of similar ability.

Competition should be *fun* and *enjoyable*. It should be seen as a challenge, but how does the serious player prepare for competition?

There are six major components required to produce a true champion who is physically fit and mentally resilient: speed, stamina, strength, skill, mental toughness, and suppleness.

SPEED

A definition of speed is 'the ratio of the distance covered to the time taken by the moving body'.

Naturally, a good tennis player needs to be fast around the court, able to get to short balls and wide balls, and also able to recover quickly after each shot. It is therefore necessary to train to improve your speed around the court. Below are a couple of footwork drills that you could try. Work as fast as possible, but do ensure you have warmed up beforehand.

Short sprints
The player runs forwards five times to the service line and then back to the baseline. Time how long this takes (see Fig. 8).

Eight ball drill
Eight balls are positioned as in Fig. 9, and the player picks up one ball at a time and returns it to his racket, which is placed on the centre mark. Time how long it takes to collect all eight balls.

Bounce and sprint
Player starts on the T-junction where the service line meets the centre service line. Stand with feet apart and bounce six times on balls of feet; sprint to any one of the eight stations, sprint back to the middle and bounce six times again. Repeat eight times in different directions (see Fig. 10).

STAMINA

This is 'the ability to withstand fatigue', which in tennis is really anything which tends to cause a deterioration in the repeated performance of the skill. A properly trained tennis player will be able to perform as well in the third or fifth set as he did in the first. A player lacking in stamina will be struggling the longer the match continues.

An easy way to increase stamina is to go on long runs, e.g. 30–60 minutes. However, the training can be more court-oriented, and a good practice is the tennis court circuit.

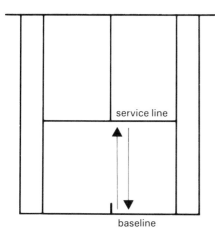

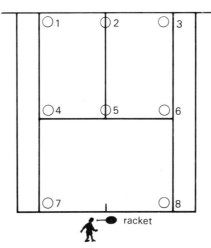

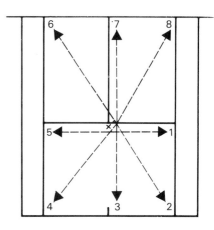

Fig. 8 **Short sprints.** *The player starts on the baseline and runs forwards to the service line. He touches the service line with his hand and returns to the baseline. This is repeated 5 times.*

Fig. 9 **Eight-ball drill.** *Tennis balls are placed at each of the eight stations 1–8. The balls are collected individually but in any order, and are placed on the racket. Time how long it takes to collect all the balls in. This practice could be performed in teams working on opposite sides of the net. The first person collects the balls, the second person puts them back again, the third person collects them, etc.*

Fig. 10 **Bounce and sprint.** *The player starts at X, bounces 6 times on the balls of his feet and sprints to one of the eight stations (1–8). He touches the ground and sprints back to X. The six bounces are repeated. He sprints to another station and back until all 8 stations have been visited.*

Tennis court circuit

Follow the route 1 to 15, running as fast as possible. Run backwards for 4–5, 6–7, 9–10, 12–13. Touch the line with your hand at each point, and at the front of the court touch the net. To improve your stamina, repeat 3–4 times (see Fig. 11).

Another easy stamina drill is shuttle running, using the width of the court.

Shuttle runs

Run to the outside sideline and back again, and repeat twelve times. Rest for one minute and then repeat. Gradually build up from 6–10 runs as your stamina improves.

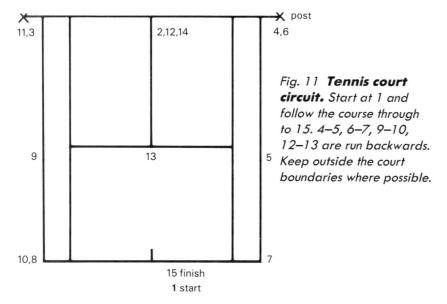

Fig. 11 **Tennis court circuit.** *Start at 1 and follow the course through to 15. 4–5, 6–7, 9–10, 12–13 are run backwards. Keep outside the court boundaries where possible.*

STRENGTH

Strength is 'the ability to exert force'. A tennis player not only needs to be quick and have stamina, but also to be strong, as force is needed to perform any action in sport.

It is unwise for young players to do weight training while they are still growing, but once a player is physically mature, weight training will help to increase strength. Added strength may be needed in the upper arms and shoulders for the serve, or in the legs for explosive movement. Strong stomach muscles are also very beneficial.

SKILL

This may be defined as 'any behaviour which tends to improve performance in tennis'.

A player may be superbly fit physically, but if his skill level is low, he will lose to a player of equal fitness but with better skills. The basic techniques of the strokes have been discussed earlier. Regular coaching lessons will help develop the skill level.

MENTAL TOUGHNESS

It is now generally agreed that once the basic techniques have been mastered, tennis is very much a game governed by mental toughness. It is most important to

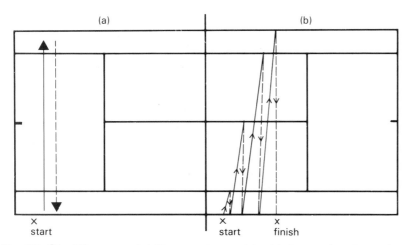

Fig. 12 **Shuttle runs.** *(a) Start on the outside sideline and sprint to the opposite sideline, touch the ground and sprint back again. (b) As a variation, start on the outside sideline and touch each line in succession, returning to start each time. Repeat 3–6 times.*

think positively and to be able to play consistently at as high a standard as you can.

Prior to competition, a player must develop all these components. He must work on his physical fitness, his skills' level and his mental approach to the game; that way he should be able to go on court and give 100% all of the time.

In the same way that an athlete prepares himself to peak for important events such as the Olympic Games, so, too, does the tennis player. Prior to competition it is therefore essential to develop a programme that encompasses physical fitness. It is no good doing a lot of stamina training two days before a major competition, only to find that your body is tired and you cannot perform to your full potential. Plan well ahead, set yourself realistic targets and then try to achieve them.

Here is an example of a simple training programme. The time span is January to March, with a major competition on 18 March on an indoor carpet (supreme surface).

This allows eleven weeks prior to the competition. During this period the player works on his physical fitness, speed, strength, stamina and suppleness, on his skills (with intensive work on any particular stroke which needs altering or modifying), and also on his mental approach.

In the first few weeks, considerable time could be spent on the physical fitness side, with a lot of weight training (specific to the individual's needs), speed work about the court (both with and without a racket), and regular stamina and suppleness sessions. Skill work would be a regular occurrence. A weekly programme might be like the one shown below.

Skills should be worked on every day, but always *before* the physical training, and this might involve 2–3 hours of practice/ conditioned match play. It is a good idea to do flexibility exercises daily. Always try to have *one day off*, as your body and mind need a rest.

As the competition draws closer, the intensity of the physical training can decrease and more emphasis can be put on strategy and tactics, points and match play, and on the mental side of the game – all specific to the needs of the individual. A large number of sets and conditioned points can be played on the same surface as that of the competition. Emphasis should be on attitude and positive thinking, so that the athlete peaks for the competition.

To summarise: in the early stages, the emphasis should be on physical fitness and technique work, moving onto strategy and tactics, with sessions on mental toughness, and finally devoting the latter stages to match play and the psychological components of competition.

SUPPLENESS

A good tennis player needs to be supple or flexible, and he also needs a good range of movement in his joints to be able to perform skills successfully. It is essential that every tennis player stretches before

Monday	Tuesday	Wednesday	Thursday	Friday	Saturday	Sunday
Suppleness	Suppleness	Suppleness	Suppleness	Suppleness	Suppleness	Rest day
Weight training	Speed and stamina	Weight training	Speed and stamina	Weight training	Competitive play	
Skills	Skills	Skills	Skills	Skills/ tactics		

playing, in the same way that an athlete spends time stretching before competition. It is a habit you should get into at an early age. If you stretch properly before play and before serious physical training, you will decrease the risk of injury and will improve mobility. Every warm-up should include some exercises for suppleness, but if you really want to improve your performance you should spend time on a full exercise programme.

Basically, there are three types of suppleness training: extension exercises; stretching exercises; and contraction – relaxation – stretching (in sequence). These exercises can be performed after your normal warm-up.

Extension exercise

Reach the maximum extended position of your arms or legs by slow, gentle pressing movements, and hold this position for approximately six seconds. Repeat about 10 times.

Stretching exercises

Hold the relaxed muscle (or group of muscles) stationary in the extended position for a further 20–60 seconds. Try to work through all the necessary joints and muscles.

Contraction – relaxation – stretching (in sequence)

This method is particularly useful for improving mobility. Fully contract a muscle or group of muscles in a partly stretched-out position for six seconds. Relax for a couple of seconds and then continue to stretch slowly to the maximum stretched-out position until you feel pressure. Hold this position for six seconds, then repeat the procedure 3–5 times. Again, work through all the muscle groups.

If you embark on a weight training programme, make sure you combine this with flexibility work to guard against shortening and stiffening of the muscles.

9 POSITIVE THINKING

Tennis contains many of the dramas of life: joy, frustration, pain, uncertainty and struggle. In order to cope with these, the player needs to be mentally fit or mentally tough. Mental strength is required in the heat of battle, e.g. at four games-all in the fifth set. Can you perform at your peak in these crucial stages of the match? Are you concentrating, thinking correctly, controlling your energy, and visualizing the match? Are you motivated? Do you have a calm attitude during this period? Are you in control of your body and mind? This is what mental toughness is all about.

A true champion is consistent, i.e. he is consistent in performance because he is psychologically consistent. He has control of his inner self, and can create a special atmosphere within himself.

There are several factors (as listed by James Loehr) which are common to all mentally-tough competitors. A mentally-tough competitor is:

a self-motivated and self-directed: he wants to be involved, everything comes from within, and nobody has to force him to participate

b positive, but very realistic: he is not a fault finder or a complainer, but a builder, an optimist and a realist

c in control of his emotions (even in situations of bad line calls, bad playing conditions, etc.): the player does not erupt in adversity, but has total control of his inner feelings

d calm and relaxed under pressure and is challenged by it; he sees tough situations not as a threat, but as an opportunity to explore his potential

e highly energised and ready for action, and is capable of getting himself 'psyched up' for matches, even when the situation might seem meaningless

f determined; he has a sheer will to succeed and achieve his goals and targets, despite any setbacks he may encounter on the way! (an excellent example of this is Jimmy Connors)

g mentally alert and focused; he is capable of long periods of concentration, and has the ability to focus on the task in hand

h self-confident; he has belief in his ability to perform, and as a result is rarely intimidated

i fully responsible for his own actions, and thus has no excuses; he realises that his destiny as a tennis player is in his own hands.

In conclusion, mentally-tough competitors have a special *inner strength*, which makes them different from the rest of us. You will always be your own toughest opponent, and once you can master yourself, mastering your opponent becomes easy.

How many times have you thought, prior to an important match, 'I hope I don't lose to him, what will everybody think?', or, 'If I lose this match, my ranking will drop', or, 'I cannot stand the pressure'? These are all negative thoughts which will not help you perform at your best.

Everybody talks about 'pressure' in tennis, the 'pressure of being seeded', the 'pressure of people expecting you to do well', etc. It is true that *nobody* performs well *under pressure*. However, skilful players perform well in what we might call 'pressure situations' simply because they actually eliminate the pressure. Try to remember one thing: *pressure is something you put on yourself.*

You might like playing tennis for fun, but see competition as too tough, too much like hard work. Do you view competition as threatening, frustrating, or unnerving? The game is played exactly the same in both cases, the rules are the same, the score is called the same way, and often you are playing the same person – so what is the difference? In most cases, the only difference is the one you make in your head! For example, to say 'one counts and the other doesn't', is to express a thought originating *in your head.*

To become a mentally-tough competitor, to stay relaxed and calm when you play and to stay in a positive frame of mind, you have to change your thought process and learn to structure your thoughts. *Mental toughness is learned, not inherited.* As soon as you accept the fact that pressure comes from inside

you, the sooner you can start to shut it out. You need to be a disciplined thinker.

> If you think you are beaten, you are;
> If you think you dare not, you don't.
> If you would like to win, but think you can't,
> It's almost certain you won't.
> If you think you'll lose, you've lost;
> For out in the world you'll find
> Success begins with a fellow's will,
> It's all in the state of mind.
> If you think you are outclassed, you are;
> You've got to think high to rise;
> You've got to be sure of yourself before
> You can ever win the prize.
> Life's battles don't always go
> To the stronger or faster man;
> But sooner or later the man who wins
> Is the man who thinks he can.
>
> Napoleon Hill, *The Law of Success*

Consider some examples of negative thoughts which will produce pressure:

> What will happen if I lose this match?

> The pressure is awful.
> I cannot play under pressure.
> What will my coach say?
> If I lose, that's it, I'm quitting.
> My ranking will slip.
> What will my friends say at school?

The mentally-tough competitor will be thinking positively:

> I'm going to give it 100% and let winning take care of itself.
> I'll just concentrate on the game and do the best I can.
> I'm going to enjoy this match.
> I love tough situations.
> This match is a challenge.
> I'm going to have fun out there.
> I'm going to perform.

In the first instance, a player sees the competition as a fearful, frustrating experience, and he is worried about losing. He is negative and pessimistic, and is likely to look for all sorts of excuses if he loses the match.

Conversely, the positive thinker sees the competition as a challenge; he is enthusiastic and inspired, and will not make excuses for failure. The only difference is how the situation is perceived in each player's head.

10 MATCH STRATEGY AND TACTICS

Firstly, it is essential to define the terms 'strategy' and 'tactics'. Strategy is the overall game plan, and tactics is the method used to outwit an opponent in implementing this plan. For example, a player's strategy might be to attack his opponent at every conceivable opportunity, and this strategy might be implemented by a tactic of serving and volleying.

As a coach, I am often asked by beginners to teach them strategy and tactics; but to be honest, until a player can hit the ball where he wants it to go, it is very hard to implement any tactics! Giving a pupil a target area to aim for does, however, help to develop his tennis game. If every alternate shot goes into the net it is difficult to use any tactics!

In the game of singles, most points are won as a result of the opponent making an error. In simple terms of tactics, therefore, you must not make an error before your opponent does! In terms of ball placement, you either go down the line or crosscourt, and the basic tactical choices are to go to the net or to stay on the baseline. Either you attack or you defend.

It all sounds very easy, but there are many variables which will influence your battle plan, and you need continually to be concentrating, analysing and anticipating to be one step ahead of your opponent. There are a number of factors which will affect your decision as to which tactics you employ:

a the abilities and skills you possess, i.e. your own style of play; this includes your strengths and weaknesses

b your opponent's style of play, including his strengths and weaknesses

c your own physical condition

d your opponent's physical condition; for example, if your opponent is slightly overweight, the chances are he will tire quickly, in which case the tactics you use involve moving your opponent around, using drop shots and lobs, and generally making sure your opponent is put under physical pressure

e the court surface you are playing on; tactics used on a fast court, e.g. grass, will differ from those on a slower surface, e.g. clay

f the climatic conditions; you would use different tactics when playing in the wind from those on a bright, still day

g the mental capacities of yourself and your opponent.

The key to successful tactics is having a degree of flexibility if and when necessary. Remember the slogan, 'Always change a losing game and never change a winning game' — it is so true. You might have a game plan when you walk out on court, but if your method of attack is back-firing, slow down, and think about why it is not working. Are you coming in after the wrong balls? Are you playing to your opponent's strengths? You must decide whether you are using the wrong tactics, or whether you have the right tactics but are not executing them correctly! Do not let your brain 'race' when you are down; take your time, gather your thoughts, look unruffled and give an air of confidence, showing you have your emotions under control.

PERCENTAGE TENNIS

I am sure you have heard the expression 'playing the percentage'; what does it mean? In laymen's terms it means hitting the shot which is most likely to give you success (usually an easy one). For example, if your opponent plays the ball crosscourt, the easiest return is another ball crosscourt. The down-the-line return is harder because you have to change the direction of the ball, and because the net is higher at the side than in the middle. Do not try to hit the flashy shot, and make an error, when a simpler, easier shot will win you the point. Try to think what your best percentage shots are, and use them. This is particularly important on big points or game points, or when you are a break down, etc.

PLAYING TO YOUR OWN STRENGTHS

As a player you must be fully aware of your own strengths and weaknesses, both physical and mental. It is essential to understand your own game and your emotions. Once you understand these, you can do something about them.

If you possess a strong forehand, use it. Steffi Graf has a phenomenally powerful forehand, and utilises her good footwork to move around the ball to hit this devastating shot. If your return of serve is your greatest asset, make good use of that. Jimmy Connors survived many years at the top flight of the game with a classic example of a great service return. If your strength is your volley, try to take control of the net at every opportunity; an example of this type of player is Martina Navratilova. If you possess a powerful serve, ensure you give yourself time to hit the shot, and get a high percentage of first serves into court, aimed at your opponent's weaker side.

Try to think to yourself: 'What is my best shot?' and work on this strength. Attempt to move your opponent around so that the ball is in a position where you can hit your best shot.

PLAYING TO YOUR OPPONENT'S WEAKNESSES

The key to good tactics is getting your opponent in a situation from which he hits his worst shot, i.e. exploiting your opponent's weaknesses. In most cases at club level, the backhand shot is the weakest one. However, if you hit every single ball onto your opponent's backhand, he could

easily establish a rhythm or, conversely, knowing the ball was coming on that side, run round it and take the shot on the forehand!

To exploit your opponent's weakness, you sometimes have to hit to his strengths, even if he possesses a really powerful shot. He might then start to become anxious and miss a few shots. Once his confidence about his best shot falters, it is very hard for him to play aggressively. Keep your opponent moving and guessing all the time.

With the majority of people it is easy to spot their weakness or weaknesses, e.g. the serve, the volley or the backhand. However, you might find with other players that their weakness is not as obvious, and you have to seek out the shots or court positions which they do not like; for example, your opponent might be tremendously quick when moving along the baseline to retrieve balls, but slow when moving forwards and backwards. Your opponent might possess very hard-hit ground strokes and consequently enjoy an oncoming hard-hit ball, but not a slower, softer ball. In these circumstances it might be better not to play to your opponent's strength, but to give him balls he hates hitting!

If possible, it is advisable before a match to watch your opponent play, so that you have an idea of his strengths and weaknesses. If you are a tournament player, you will study the draw to see who you are likely to face in each round, and then take each match as it comes. Try to watch your likely opponents. If it is not possible to scout your opponent prior to the match, you need to spot his weaknesses as early as possible in the game. This will begin in the knock-up.

A nervous player will be very stiff and immobile, resembling a robot. If you are like this, chase every ball in the knock-up, to help loosen your tensed muscles. Another idea to control your nerves is to hit a few shots with maximum power; this might help you to stroke the ball smoothly. During the knock-up, test your opponent out a little; move him around, find out what he is like against wide balls, hard balls, soft balls, balls with spin, volleys and smashes. See how hard, and to which part of the court, he serves. This will give you a few ideas.

I can remember watching two juniors prepare for their match, going through the rituals of a few volleys and smashes in the knock-up; when one of the boys was at the net, his opponent asked, 'Do you want a few smashes?', to which the other replied: 'No . . . I never hit any in a match!' A similar experience might just tell you of an area to exploit!

Once the match starts, test your opponent out to see how he handles various situations; you should soon be able to exploit a weakness. Be prepared to experiment further as the match progresses, as weaknesses can often surface at a later stage of the match.

BASELINE TACTICS

A good baseliner will hit the ball about 60 to 90 cm (24 to 35 in) above the net, to give a good margin for error and make it easy to hit the ball to a good length. Most errors consist of balls going into the net, so play the percentage shot.

A baseliner will understand how to open up the court and draw a short ball from his opponent in order to make the kill. One of the best baseliners of all time is Chris Evert, who in her prime was very consistent and solid with her ground strokes, making hardly any unforced errors.

A good baseliner will move his opponent around the court and vary his shots in order to keep the opponent guessing. This means not only moving him from side to side along the baseline (some players are excellent at this) but also forwards and backwards so that the length and breadth of the court are used. Sidelines can be used to take an opponent out of court.

There are two types of baseliners: those who are defensive and those who are aggressive. The defensive baseliner will keep the ball in play until the opponent makes an error, i.e. he will hit a certain number of shots until the opponent gets frustrated, panics and therefore misses the shot. This type of defensive player (or retriever) is generally quite fit, particularly if he is to retrieve for a whole match! The aggressive baseliner will hit more to the corners, and when the opponent hits a short ball will attack the opening with a ground stroke.

If you are a baseliner, you must vary your shots: use the different spins (topspin, flat and slice), and vary the pace of the ball. If you consistently hit shots at the same pace, it is easy for your opponent to get into your rhythm of play. Accelerate the racket head through the ball occasionally to generate more pace, hit some loopy topspin or use the drop shot; keep your opponent guessing.

The easiest shot to hit from the baseline is the crosscourt ball, because the net is lower in the middle than at the sides, and the ball travels a great distance. In addition, a crosscourt drive can be hit with an open stance. It is a natural swing to hit crosscourt, and you have wide angles to exploit.

When hitting down the line, take

your time, because the net is higher at the sidelines, and ensure you turn. Do not aim for the line, but rather well inside it. Although a player can get away with hitting the ball late when attempting to play crosscourt (the ball will still go into court), a late contact when hitting down the line will result in the ball landing in the side lines.

If scurrying for a ball, do not be afraid to throw up a high lob to give yourself time to recover, and to disrupt your opponent's rhythm. This is a very sound, sensible tactic.

SERVE-AND-VOLLEY TACTICS

If you possess a good serve and you like to volley, you might use the serve-and-volley tactic with regularity. Serving and volleying is naturally more effective on a fast court surface than on a slow one, because the ball rebounded will be quicker and the ball can be put away more easily. Martina Navratilova is one of the best female serve-and-volleyers of modern times, while Boris Becker achieved his successes at Wimbledon with devastating use of these tactics. This type of player will approach the net whenever possible: positioning oneself close to the net has both a physical and a psychological advantage.

A good serve-and-volleyer will vary his serve so that his opponent is never sure about what to expect. This means altering the type of spin and the direction of the ball. To be effective with this tactic, it is important to follow the serve into the net as quickly as possible, so that your opponent is hurried into making a return and consequently forced into making an error.

One of the keys to effective serve-and-volley tactics is to use the 'check step' when coming into the net. When approaching the net, the server has to stop momentarily at the same time as the receiver strikes the ball, in order to be well balanced and to react to the receiver's return. If the server does not use the 'split step' (the player jumps slightly off one foot to land on two), it is very difficult to change direction and suddenly move to the left or to the right. The end result is

that the server finds it hard to hit a good first volley. At a lower level this often means the first volley ends up over the baseline because the ball has been played late with an open racket face while the server is still on the run. An accomplished serve-and-volleyer will be 'splitting' near the service line, playing his first volley from this position and then moving closer to the net for the next one.

In the early stages of learning to serve-and-volley it is advisable to practise with a slower or topspin serve, because this will give you more time to get to the net. Another important point to remember is to follow the path of the ball to cover the angles of the service return. For example, if you serve wide from the right court you position yourself as in the diagram below.

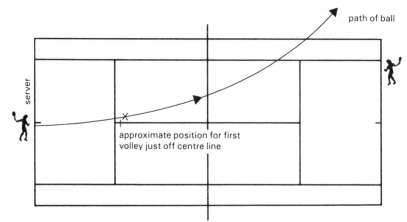

Fig. 13 Serving and volleying: if the player serving from the right court serves wide, he follows the path of the ball and plays the first volley from X. He then moves closer to the net for the next volley.

Serving wide will obviously open up the court for an easy volley, but it does give the receiver more angles for the return. Serving down the centre line will limit the server's angles for volleys, but it reduces the area into which the receiver can play the ball. An effective server will use both of these options and will also serve some balls into the receiver's body. In doubles play, the serve down the centre line is favoured.

If you do not possess a very good second serve, it is inadvisable to follow the second delivery into the net, because your opponent will invariably be thinking positively and will be ready to attack any weak delivery. Likewise, if you are not serving very well, it is a sound tactic to fake a rush to the net and to stay on the baseline and then come in off the first short ball. Once you get to the net, make your opponent run to retrieve your volleys, as he will be far less effective on the run with his passing shots and lobs. Serving and volleying can be great fun, particularly if you are quick at the net and you cover the possible angles of return.

TACTICS WHEN THE OPPONENT IS AT THE NET

Once your opponent is at the net, whether it be after the serve or after an approach shot, the golden rule is: 'make your opponent play the ball', i.e. force your opponent to hit a winning shot. At club level, all too often the net player does not even have to hit a ball because the return either goes into the net or sails out over the baseline. Avoid giving your opponent the point with a needless error, and do not be tempted to hit the ball very hard on your passing shots when a simple, basic forehand or backhand drive would be sufficient.

Most passing shots should be hit with topspin, because this will cause the ball to dip and so keep low once it has passed the net. It also forces the volleyer to hit the ball upwards. Vary your passing shots so that the volleyer cannot predict where the ball will go. If the volleyer is standing too far away from the net, try passing crosscourt and aim for the short corner (where the service line meets the side line). If the volleyer is very close to the net, it is easier to pass down the line. Again, play to your opponent's weakness. As an element of surprise, you could also try a shot aimed directly at your opponent, which often forces an error.·

The lob is highly effective when the volleyer is on top of the net. Here you could use an attacking topspin lob. It is also useful when you are forced to hit from a very deep position, or a wide position – in which case you would use a high defensive lob, allowing you time to recover your court position or even to get into an advantageous court position.

If playing against a serve-and-volleyer, return the ball low over the net at the server's feet. It is tactically sound to take the ball early, thereby forcing the server to volley a little bit earlier than he would like. Another good tactic to employ is to 'chip and charge', and so get to the net before the server does. Try this initially against an opponent with a weak second serve. When the server is looking up at his toss, that is the time to start moving forwards (the server cannot see you, because he is watching the ball). Take the ball early, let the momentum carry you to the net and then hit your normal volleys.

HOW TO PLAY THE SOFT BALLER

I am sure you have played against opponents who hit with no pace, but who nevertheless consistently return the ball. This type of player is probably the most frustrating person you have to face, and all too often you fall into his trap: you start to overswing, you are lured into his pace of ball, you become bored and frustrated, and you lose concentration. You might even lose your cool and, as a result, the match.

The keys to playing such an opponent are patience and common sense: patience, because you need to know when to hold back and when to attack; and common sense, because generally this player has no winning shots, but simply forces you to beat yourself. Stay calm and continue to think clearly.

Although there may be no pace on the ball, it does not mean you should stroll around the court; you must still prepare early and get to the ball in good time so that you can force your opponent to hurry his return. It is imperative that you break up your opponent's rhythm, rather than getting lulled into his style of play. One tactic you could use is to approach the net whenever possible and put the volley away.

Do be prepared for several lobs, too! It might be a good idea to practise your smash before the match! Try coming into the court and volleying some of the higher midcourt balls. Use the serve-and-volley tactic, but move quickly to the net. Returns should be hit deep or angled, but make sure you do not make silly errors on soft serves; step in and meet the ball. Remember to play the ball, not your opponent, and don't beat yourself!

HOW TO PLAY THE HARD HITTER

No doubt you prefer to play the hard power hitter rather than the soft baller. Many people, though, are intimidated by the hard hitter and actually 'psyche' themselves out of the match before it even starts. Watch the ball, and not your opponent's big wind-up. Play your own game and not his. If you become caught up in a power hitting contest, you will invariably lose, because your opponent will just hit the ball even harder!

If your opponent likes pace, try not to give it to him. Put up some loopy topspin shots, and hit a few lobs or gentle drop shots to break up his rhythm – play to your strengths. If your opponent is serving very hard, use the pace on the ball and block the return with a shortened backswing. If you can take the ball early, you nullify your opponent's biggest weapon. Alternatively, you can stand further behind the baseline so that the ball has lost some of its strength by the time it reaches you. Do not play the rest of the match from this position, though; take up your normal ready position.

Generally, the hard hitter likes short points, so the longer you can stay on court with him, the better the chance of your winning.

HOW TO PLAY IMPORTANT POINTS

No doubt you have been told to play one point at a time and to play in the present, not the past or the future. This is correct: focus on the point in question. Some points, however, are more important than others, and it is essential for a player to recognise these:

a to win the first point of every game has the psychological advantage of 'getting the upper hand' over your opponent

b when serving, if you are 15–30 or 0–30 down, the next point is vital, as it could mean a service break

c as soon as one player reaches 40, the next point is important, because it is a game point

d quite often in a match a player has a very close first set, and then the score is 6–0 in the second; after a tight first set, concentrate very hard on the first few games in the next one

e likewise, if you win the first set easily, keep playing hard in the second and maintain concentration, rather than letting complacency set in.

You probably think of the big points as the game points, break points, etc. It is important to play the percentage shot on these occasions, rather than trying for the spectacular winner. For example, make sure that your first serve goes into court on important points, even if it is only hit at 80% of your maximum power; this is better than 100% power for 40% consistency, and needless extra pressure on yourself (having to hit a second serve). Use your strengths to the full on the crucial points. Do not aim unnecessarily for the lines when a shot 60 cm (24 in) from the line, with more margin for error, would suffice.

Think positively on these points. Concentrate hard. Relax, slow down and take a couple of deep breaths. Above all, play the percentage shot and make your opponent play the ball.

CLIMATIC CONDITIONS

When playing outside, the tactics employed will depend on the various climatic conditions in which you are playing.

Wind

Playing in the wind is always very difficult, because you can be faced not only with a downcourt wind, but also a crosscourt or a swirling one, and because of the unpredictability of the wind you will need considerable concentration. In the warm-up period you should note very carefully the strength and direction of the wind. You can then use it to your advantage. For example, if there is a crosscourt wind you could slice the ball out wide, and the wind will carry it

even further away from your opponent.

When playing in the wind it is essential to contact the ball solidly, and to hit through the ball so that the ball–racket contact is as long as possible. Always follow through with the racket pointing in the direction in which you want the ball to go. Prepare early with the racket, and keep a short backswing; this will help if you are uncertain as to the actual path of the ball.

If hitting with the wind, it is advisable to hit with topspin, because the spin will cause the ball to dip and so prevent unnecessary errors over the baseline. If hitting against the wind, you can afford to hit the ball harder; you need to hit it firmly so that the wind does not dramatically change the path of the ball. A topspin drive will cause the ball to dip and stay low after crossing the net, whilst a ball off a sliced drive will tend to float and hang in the air. If you want to hit drop shots, hit them against the wind, because they will be very effective, and will possibly even bounce back over the net into your own half. Drop shots hit with the wind will be suicidal!

When playing with the wind, come into the net, because your opponent's shots will be slowed down and you can readily get yourself into an advantageous

attacking position. If you come into the net after a good serve or a good, clean approach shot, your opponent will find it hard to pass you, and any lob will tend to hang in the air. Lobs hit with the wind are hard to control, as the ball will travel further than normal. Lobs hit against the wind can be hit harder and higher.

Serving is often very difficult in the wind, particularly if you have a high place up, as the wind will move the ball around too much. It is advantageous to have a lower place up. The ball should still be contacted at your maximum reach, but the lower toss ensures the ball will not be subjected to influences of the wind. Although playing in the wind is hard, many of the problems of players are self-inflicted because of negative attitudes, e.g. 'I hate playing in the wind', or 'I cannot serve in the wind'. If a player takes a positive attitude, looking at the windy conditions as a challenge and concentrating very hard on the path of the ball, playing in these conditions can be enjoyable.

Sun

Most players prefer sunny conditions to windy conditions, and there are basic tactics you can utilise on bright, sunny days. If the sun is shining directly into your opponent's eyes, put up a high lob. This is very difficult to smash; the only sensible option is to let the ball bounce and move into a position so that the sun is not in your eyes. After looking directly at a bright light, the eyes take time to focus again, and at a lower level this could result in an error in the smash.

The sun can also pose problems to the server if it shines directly into a player's eyes. This can be alleviated by:

a modifying the server's stance (by opening or closing it more)

b altering the server's position along the baseline

c altering the direction of the ball placement slightly.

VARIED COURT SURFACES

In the same way that there are different types of rackets and strings, there are also various court surfaces, each of which requires different tennis tactics because of the different ball rebound heights and speeds. For example, on a clay court there is a slower rebound than on a cement court, where there is a harder texture and resulting quicker rebound. Different types of surface suit different styles of player.

Basically, there are three types of surface to be aware of:

a fast surfaces, e.g. wood, grass, cement

b slow surfaces, e.g. clay or clay types

c medium surfaces – all others (including many indoor surfaces).

Fast surfaces

Fast surfaces suit serve-and-volleyers and aggressive players. Boris Becker, for example, is far more effective on grass than on clay. The characteristics of a fast surface, e.g. grass, are that the ball will rebound quickly and stay low. A player therefore needs to prepare very early, and short backswings on strokes are best if the ball is coming through quickly. Tactically, a hard flat or slice serve, if well placed, will be a useful asset. A player must move quickly into position, as the ball will be coming through faster, and if hit with slice it will tend to skid through. If playing on cement, again a fast surface, the ball will rebound off the surface quickly, but will bounce appreciably higher than on grass. This surface will again suit a serve-and-volley style player, but there will not be that degree of uncertainty on the bounce that is characteristic of grass.

Slow surfaces

Conversely, the ball rebound on a clay court is much slower and higher. This surface will suit the consistent baseliner. A serve-and-volleyer will not be as effective on clay, because it is far more difficult to put the ball away for a winner. A baseliner is in his element on clay: he can hit with loopy topspin, giving the ball height over the net, and have ample time for a full backswing.

One important quality for a successful clay court player is *patience*, because the rallies are longer and you need to work harder to win the points. Tactically, you must hit to a length and with accuracy, and wait for the opening before trying to win the point. If you attempt too many flashy shots, you will end up on a 'hiding to nothing' against the consistent baseliner. Be prepared for a long match, as your best shots may well come floating back over the net.

One of the most notable successes in recent years of an aggressive player winning on clay is Yannick Noah, who won the French Open in 1983. Noah attacked the net on every conceivable occasion. As a rule, it is those players with solid ground strokes who dominate on clay, e.g. Mats Wilander.

Medium surfaces

A medium surface suits the serve-and-volleyer as well as the baseliner. Some of the most intriguing matches to watch and analyse are when a serve-and-volleyer is playing against a baseliner, for example, Chris Evert against Martina Navratilova.

GLOSSARY

Backhand Stroke played with the racket across the front of the body and the back of the hand facing the front.

Block Type of action used on the volley. Little takeback with the racket and little follow-through.

Checkstep Player moves from one foot to land on two feet as he slows down prior to contacting the ball. Used considerably when serving and volleying prior to hitting the ball.

Closed racket face Head of racket is tilted downwards, with strings facing slightly downwards; used when hitting topspin drives.

Conditioned match play Match play involving some form of stipulated practice.

Cool-down Method of helping body to return to normality after vigorous exercise.

Drill Method of training by repetition of exercises.

Drive Ball which is hit after the bounce.

Follow-through Continuation of the stroke after hitting the ball.

Forehand Stroke played with the palm of the hand facing the front.

Grip Method of holding the racket.

Groundstroke A collective term for the forehand and backhand drives.

Let Service in which the ball touches the top of the net before landing in the correct service box.

Lift Term used to describe the path of the ball on the backhand when the ball is hit to a high level to get it over the net.

Lob Ball which is hit high into the air.

Net play Refers to all shots played near the net, e.g. volleys and their variations, and the smash.

Open racket face Head of the racket is tilted slightly upwards, with strings facing upwards.

Open stance Refers to a groundstroke. Player is positioned facing the net. (Often used when hitting a topspin forehand.)

Place-up/toss Method of putting the ball lightly into the air by the hand on the serve.

Point of impact Refers to the exact place at which the ball meets the racket strings.

Punch Type of action used on the volley.

Ready position Position from which a player starts, prior to contacting or moving to the ball.

Service Act of striking the ball to start play.

Short tennis A scaled-down version of lawn tennis, played on a smaller court with a lower net and either plastic or strung rackets and foam or transition balls.

Shuttle-run Moving backwards and forwards between two places.

Smash Shot used to counteract the lob. Generally hit hard with a powerful throwing action.

Soft baller Player who hits with little pace on his shots.

Stance Position of player when about to strike the ball.

Strategy Overall plan or method for winning the match.

Swing Path of the racket on groundstrokes.

Takeback Method of moving the racket back from the body on various strokes.

Throwing action Path of the racket on the service and smash.

Volley Name given to the shot in which the ball is hit before the bounce.

Warm-up Method of preparing the body prior to vigorous activity.

INDEX